The
Genius
— *of* —
Athletes

The Genius of Athletes

of Athletes

What World-Class Competitors Know
That Can Change Your Life

NOEL BRICK, PhD
SCOTT DOUGLAS

THE EXPERIMENT

NEW YORK

THE GENIUS OF ATHLETES: *What World-Class Competitors Know That Can Change Your Life*
Copyright © 2021 by Noel Brick, PhD, and Scott Douglas

The Experiment, LLC
220 East 23rd Street, Suite 600
New York, NY 10001-4658
theexperimentpublishing.com

THE EXPERIMENT and its colophon are registered trademarks of The Experiment, LLC. Many of the designations used by manufacturers and sellers to distinguish their products are claimed as trademarks. Where those designations appear in this book and The Experiment was aware of a trademark claim, the designations have been capitalized.

The Experiment's books are available at special discounts when purchased in bulk for premiums and sales promotions as well as for fundraising or educational use. For details, contact us at info@theexperimentpublishing.com.

Library of Congress Cataloging-in-Publication Data

Names: Brick, Noel, author. | Douglas, Scott, 1964- author.
Title: The genius of athletes : what world-class competitors know that can change your life / Noel Brick, PhD, Scott Douglas.
Description: New York : The Experiment, LLC, [2021]
Identifiers: LCCN 2021006729 (print) | LCCN 2021006730 (ebook) | ISBN 9781615196418 | ISBN 9781615196425 (ebook)
Subjects: LCSH: Athletes--Conduct of life. | Success. | Sports--Psychological aspects.
Classification: LCC GV706.55 .B75 2021 (print) | LCC GV706.55 (ebook) | DDC 796.01/9--dc23
LC record available at https://lccn.loc.gov/2021006729
LC ebook record available at https://lccn.loc.gov/2021006730

ISBN 978-1-61519-641-8
Ebook ISBN 978-1-61519-642-5

Jacket and text design by Jack Dunnington
Author photographs by Nigel McDowell/Ulster University (Noel Brick) and Stacey Cramp (Scott Douglas)

Manufactured in the United States of America

First printing May 2021
10 9 8 7 6 5 4 3 2 1

For Dr. P. J. Smyth, an inspiration and role model who laid the foundations for this book by generously sharing his passion for sport psychology.

Contents

———

PART 2

How to Reach Any Goal
Like an Elite Athlete

Introduction

———

It's time for the dumb jock to retire.

We're not talking about a particular athletic lunkhead. We mean the idea of the dumb jock, the stereotype of all-brawn, no-brain athletes who muscle their way through training and competition with an empty mind. The truth is, top athletes are constantly thinking. As we'll see throughout this book, what they're specifically thinking about varies depending on a vast number of conditions. But the goal of their thinking is this: "How can I best use my physical and mental resources to get the most out of myself?" The ones who frequently answer that correctly are the ones who more often than not prevail over their peers.

Of course, if you work out regularly, you're also thinking a lot while in motion. But do those thoughts always help you to succeed? Research, including that done by one of this book's authors, Noel Brick, consistently finds that elite athletes employ a few key psychological tools. These ways of thinking are far more sophisticated than the suck-it-up clichés so often associated with athletes. Top athletes have unique ways of taking stock of a situation, of talking to themselves, even of thinking about time. They have a tool kit of these techniques, and they know which to use when navigating challenging situations in training and competition.

The good news is that these psychological techniques can be learned. As we'll see, even the world's top athletes pick up these practices over years of personal experience and learning from other athletes, coaches, and sport psychologists. This book will help you to significantly shorten that learning curve. You'll find that being able to think like an athlete is a game changer. We'll show you which tools are most effective, and how best to use them in several typical challenging situations—when you're starting something seemingly overwhelming, when you're struggling to maintain motivation, when you want to quit, and so on. These tools are key to succeeding both in the moment and over the course of long-term undertakings.

REAL-WORLD APPLICATIONS

Once learned, these psychological tools can be used in daily life. In these pages you'll hear how athletes, from Olympians to everyday exercisers, have applied these tools to managing all sorts of non-sport endeavors: leading a team at a large financial services firm, battling cancer, succeeding in school, helping a community through a public health crisis, growing a start-up business, and more.

Sport can help us learn many important skills needed to navigate these real-life situations. Sport can teach us how to set and achieve goals, solve problems, cope with stress, manage our emotions, refocus after mistakes, and build self-confidence.[1] By participating in sport, we come to appreciate the value of effort, perseverance, and teamwork.

We learn about the importance of showing respect for others and taking responsibility for our own actions. Research has shown that these personal and social skills, learned through sport participation, can transfer to help us in other areas of our lives, even without a caring coach or thoughtful parent explicitly telling us how.[2]

Moreover, sports that require us to demonstrate specific qualities to succeed, such as the high level of commitment required to complete a marathon, the emotional control needed in a tight basketball game, or the perseverance and sustained focus demanded throughout a Brazilian jiujitsu contest, can help us to acquire some vital life skills.[3] The growing body of knowledge about how sport can develop transferable life skills has given rise to many programs with an explicit focus on using sport, and the mental skills learned through sport, to foster life-skill development in people of all ages.

The US-based nonprofit organization Girls on the Run, for example, uses running and other physical activities as a platform to teach life skills and promote healthy behaviors to third- through eighth-grade girls.[4] One program tailored for third- through fifth-grade girls, also called Girls on the Run, includes strategies that help these girls set goals, manage their emotions, express how they feel, and stand up for themselves. After completing the ten-week program, girls reported growth in important life skills, including improved abilities to manage their emotions, for example, by calming themselves if they felt frustrated or angry, to solve conflicts and disagreements, to stand up for others, and to think through important decisions.[5] These benefits appear to be long-lasting, too. When researchers followed up three months after the program ended, participants reported that these life-skill improvements were sustained, even though they'd had no further life-skill lessons during that time.[6]

Or consider Ahead of the Game, a sports-club-based mental health program founded in Australia for twelve- to seventeen-year-old boys.[7] Two components of the program were specifically developed for boys of that age. The first, Help Out a Mate, is a group workshop that educates on mental health issues, teaching participants how to recognize signs of depression and anxiety, encourage help seeking, and understand self-help behaviors. The second, Your Path to Success in Sport, consists of a single workshop followed by a series of brief online modules that teach the mental skills that elite athletes use—the ones presented throughout this book—to overcome adversity and build resilience.[8] These mental skills include problem-solving, focusing on controllable actions, and managing thoughts and emotions. Teaching these skills has resulted in many positive benefits for program participants, including greater awareness of signs of mental health issues, increased well-being, and improved psychological resilience, not just in sport but, more importantly, in their day-to-day lives.[9]

Other programs have focused on teaching the mental techniques used by elite athletes to individuals in non-sport settings. These programs have shown that, even for people with no sporting background, learning these skills can improve the participants' lives. One such project is My Strengths Training for Life (MST4Life), a ten-week program led by a team of researchers based at the University of Birmingham in the United Kingdom.[10]

Developed in conjunction with St. Basils, a youth homelessness charity in the West Midlands region of England, MST4Life focuses on young people who are not employed or enrolled in education or job training. The program is aimed at helping young homeless people develop life skills and, in doing so, build resilience, enhance feelings of self-worth and well-being, and, ultimately, reengage with society. Program activities include the strengths-profiling exercise we present in the first appendix, designed to increase awareness of personal psychological strengths, and weekly follow-up sessions that develop mental techniques and skills like goal setting, planning how to overcome challenges, managing emotions, dealing with stressful events, and building resilience.[11] A recent evaluation of the program has shown that when young people identified their character strengths, it helped to increase feelings of resilience, self-worth, and well-being.[12] In other words, becoming more aware of your strengths and weaknesses, and developing them using the tools presented in this book, can have an important impact on many areas of your life. And as MST4Life has shown, you don't have to be a successful athlete to gain these benefits. You just need to learn how to think like one.

TOOLS AND THEIR BEST USES

As we said, we like to think of these psychological techniques as tools in a kit. As with any tool kit, there are two keys to using it: knowing how to operate each tool, and knowing when is best to turn to that tool rather than the others in your kit.

We've structured this book around that concept. In part 1, we'll describe five key psychological tools that athletes use to get the most out of themselves. These tools help them to set and achieve goals, regulate their emotions, enhance their focus, change their self-talk, and build their self-confidence. (These things might sound obvious, but as we'll see, the way successful athletes use these tools is anything but ordinary.) In part 2, we'll proceed through the common stages of a challenging situation, and show which combination of tools to use to best navigate each stage.

We want to emphasize again that the scenarios in part 2 apply both to athletic endeavors and to everyday life. Whatever Noel and coauthor Scott Douglas have accomplished in our professional lives—a PhD and widely cited research for Noel, books on *The New York Times* bestseller list for Scott—these achievements stem in large part from the psychological tools we acquired and honed as lifelong athletes.

As you read about the tools and how to use them, you'll probably find yourself comparing how you approach challenges with how top athletes do. That reflection is helpful. If you want to take that self-discovery a little deeper, we have a fun exercise for you in appendix 1 that's based on the strengths-profiling tool we mentioned earlier. It will help make you more aware of your own mental qualities, and identify which are strengths and which are areas that can be improved by learning and applying different strategies. Feel free to create your strengths profile at any time while reading this book.

We're excited to share what we and others have learned about the life-changing benefits of thinking like an athlete. So let's get going!

PART 1

The Toolbox
of Psychological
Techniques

CHAPTER 1

Success Starts Here

The Goal-Setting and Goal-Striving Tools

———

WORLD-RENOWNED BIOLOGIST BERND HEINRICH is known for fascinating research on topics such as how bumblebees share food and how unrelated ravens communicate. In our opinion, however, one of his most important contributions has been proposing a theory that can't be proved.

Long before Christopher McDougall's bestseller *Born to Run* popularized the idea that long-distance running played an important role in human evolution, Heinrich published a book called *Why We Run*. The book's original title, *Racing the Antelope*, gives a better hint of Heinrich's central idea: Humans' ancestral history of persistence hunting, or chasing down prey until it collapsed, has had a lasting effect on our minds. "We are psychologically evolved to pursue long-range goals, because through millions of years that is what we on average had to do in order to eat,"[1] Heinrich wrote.

In this view, being fully human means working toward challenging long-term goals. Heinrich calls them "substitute chases." For him, that has meant achievements in research and running, including holding American records for 100 kilometers and 100 miles. Your substitute chases might include any number of athletic endeavors, as well as ambitious life goals—earning a degree, launching a new product, creating a work of art.

Often, our problem isn't setting goals. Daydreaming is easy and fun. What many of us find more difficult is continuing to strive to achieve them. As we'll see, where athletes get a head start is in setting, and focusing on, the right types of goals to begin with. In doing so, they set the stage to use their special thinking skills to achieve those goals. In this chapter, we'll look at how to succeed at both stages of a substitute chase: goal setting and goal striving.

NOT ALL GOALS ARE CREATED EQUAL

Let's begin with some goal-setting basics. When we think about our personal goals, and all the actions required to achieve them, we can break them down into three interconnected types: outcome goals, performance goals, and process goals.

Outcome goals are the focus of our ambitions and the end result of our actions. They might include winning a competition, graduating from college, or losing weight.

Performance goals help us achieve these outcomes. Winning a competition or graduating from college requires a certain level of performance, like running a personal best time or consistently getting adequate grades. Equally, we might put a figure on our weight-loss target. Performance goals help us know how to act and give us a measurable standard against which we can gauge our progress. If these goals are realistic and achievable, this is OK.

Process goals are what we'll do to meet our performance goals, activity that, in turn, leads to meeting our outcome goals. Think of process goals as building blocks—our preparation, how we think, the things we say to ourselves, and what we physically do to achieve a level of performance.

This might sound familiar so far. After all, most of us have set goals like these at some point in our life. But here's the important bit: When we set goals, and begin work to achieve them, most of us focus on outcome and performance goals. We think about the end result (outcome goal) and, by doing so, lose sight of the steps we need to take to get there (process goals). In some ways, this is like going on a journey without a route planner. And because of this, many of our goal-setting journeys end right back where they started. This isn't how the best athletes go about things.

Although outcome goals are motivating, they're much less controllable than process goals. As a result, thinking too much about outcome goals when we perform can induce anxiety and be distracting.[2] Imagine a golfer who tells herself, "I need to sink this putt to win," or the student who thinks about the implications of passing—or failing—when sitting for an exam. For both, focusing on the end result, and the tension it brings, will likely lessen their chances of a successful outcome.

In contrast, top athletes focus on the process—the step-by-step actions they must take to achieve ambitious targets. Applying this approach, both the golfer and the student might use some mental strategies to help them stay relaxed and focused in the moment. Doing so will increase their chances of performing at their best and achieving the outcome they desire.

Such mental processes are the focus of this book, including the tools you need to stay calm and focused under pressure, build your self-confidence, and stay positive when your inner voice is telling you, "I can't do this." The question of what successful athletes think about has intrigued and motivated Noel and Scott throughout our careers. This, combined with a curiosity to understand how athletes' thinking skills can help in other areas of life, led us to write this book.

To answer our questions, we set ourselves learning goals[3]; that is, goals focused on learning the step-by-step processes that athletes implement to achieve extraordinary performances and outcomes. We encourage you to do the same, and journey with us as we present what we discovered by researching and speaking with successful athletes. We'll also explore how these strategies can be applied to many areas of life. These range from the major life ambitions we listed earlier, to everyday challenges we all aspire to but often fall short of achieving, such as exercising more frequently, making healthier food choices, and speaking with confidence at work. Whatever your end destination, or however ambitious your goal, the journey begins with a single step.

CHUNK IT: TAKING YOUR FIRST STEPS

Many athletes set a combination of outcome, performance, process, and learning goals. But they also break bigger, longer-term goals into a series of more manageable, shorter-term chunks or sub-goals. Take the approach of three-time major golf champion Rory McIlroy as an example:

You set goals in a number of ways. I think you can set result-oriented [outcome] goals where it's a long-term goal, or you can set little short-term goals to help you get to that long-term goal. So, instead of saying, "I want to win the Masters," I'll say, "What will help me win the Masters [process goals] and what do I need to improve to get there [learning goals]?"[4]

One way of mentally breaking up a bigger, harder-to-reach goal is to use a technique called *chunking*. Similar to McIlroy's strategy of setting short-term goals, when we chunk, we set sub-goals that, when pieced together, help us achieve a longer-term ambition.

Even for experienced athletes, focusing on smaller steps can make potentially overwhelming tasks feel more manageable. We like the approach taken by one Olympic marathoner whom Noel interviewed in a study exploring what elite runners think about during races:

> You cannot stand at the start line of a marathon and go, "I am going to run 26.2 miles today." You'd go insane! So I break it into really small chunks. I break it into five-mile chunks, and I think, "How will I feel when I get to 10 miles?" Especially in a [13.1-mile] half marathon, I have this point at eight miles where I say to myself, "I'm nearly at 10."[5]

What athletes like Rory McIlroy and this Olympic marathoner have learned is that combining short- and long-term targets can lead to better performance than focusing on bigger, long-term goals alone.[6] Research supports this practice. Setting and achieving short-term sub-goals boosts our belief and increases our longer-term persistence because doing so lets us know we're making good progress; that's useful feedback we don't always get when we set only more distant, long-term goals.[7]

This advice comes with a word of caution, however. Sometimes, when we achieve a sub-goal, we can get complacent and fall short of our longer-term target. The solution—and the reason that outcome goals remain an important part of the goal-setting mix—is to periodically remind ourselves that short-term achievements are part of a bigger, more ambitious target that we're aspiring to reach.

On the other hand, falling short of a sub-goal can be demotivating and lead us to think that we're incapable of reaching a much larger ambition. In this instance, it can help to keep our focus on the smaller picture, flexibly readjust our goals, and set new performance, process, or learning targets to help get ourselves back on track.[8]

DON'T JUST THINK IT, INK IT

Although most of us set goals, for many of us these ambitions stay solely within our mind. We conjure them up, but we don't write them down. But as athletes have learned, penning our goals can be a powerful motivational tool.

Take the example of a New Zealander named Richie McCaw. Growing up in North Otago during the 1980s and '90s, McCaw held ambitions similar to those of many New Zealand kids his age. As a talented rugby union player at age seventeen, he dreamed of becoming a future All Black, a player for the New Zealand senior international team. Navigating the path to All Black status wouldn't be easy. In New Zealand there are more than 150,000 registered rugby union players, or about 3 percent of the New Zealand population. The corresponding figure in other competitive rugby union nations, such as South Africa, Ireland, England, and Australia, is about 1 percent.[9]

When McCaw discussed his dreams with his family, his uncle, John McLay, asked him to write down the steps he needed to take to realize his long-term ambition of becoming an All Black. Sitting in a restaurant one afternoon in 1998, McCaw and McLay wrote a series of career milestones on a paper napkin.[10] These included playing for the New Zealand under-nineteen age group before the end of 1999, followed by the national under-twenty-one side in 2001. He also targeted playing Super Rugby, the highest club-level standard, with the Canterbury Crusaders by 2003. If he achieved each of those milestones, he would then set himself the goal of becoming an All Black by 2004.

But why stop at that? Channeling his nephew's ambitions, McLay challenged the teenager to aim higher. He urged his nephew to set the goal of becoming not "just" an All Black but a *great* All Black—to focus on becoming one of the best players ever to represent his country. Too embarrassed to sign the paper "Great All Black" as his uncle suggested, McCaw instead abbreviated his ultimate ambition at the end of the napkin: "G.A.B."

Kicking off an international career that spanned 148 games, McCaw made his All Black debut, against Ireland, ahead of time, in 2001. Before retiring in 2015, he had twice captained New Zealand to win the Rugby World Cup and was selected as the World Rugby Player of the Year three times. He also recorded the highest number of wins and the most games as captain. He is widely considered the greatest All Black of all time.[11]

His progress highlights the value of a goal-setting principle that most of us overlook, but that many successful athletes adhere to: Write them down.[12] Charting your short-term and long-term aims will provide you with focus and direction, especially when things don't pan out as you hoped. As we'll see in chapter 2, McCaw's progress, and that of his All Black teammates, wasn't as smooth and linear as this condensed version of his story might suggest.

HOW GOOD CAN I GET?

Most of Richie McCaw's career goals aligned with expert advice on goal setting, in that they were specific, challenging but realistic, measurable, and attached to a time limit.[13] For example, the goal "play for the New Zealand under-nineteen side before the end of 1999" met all those criteria for the talented teen. It also helped McCaw direct his attention toward the what-I-need-to-do processes required to reach that level.

Possibly the most intriguing goal, however, is the ultimate "Great All Black" ambition. After all, how do you measure "great"? And how do you know when you've achieved it? You might associate the phrase "chasing great"—the title of a 2016 documentary on McCaw's life and career—with a race without a finish line, an unrelenting pursuit of dreams that are always just beyond grasp.

But maybe that's the point. Striving to achieve a fixed target that lies beyond our current reach can feel overwhelming. For a seventeen-year-old, thinking about a vaguely defined "Great All Black," and finding his own path to that ambition, probably felt less weighty than a specific standard such as "win more games than any other player in history." The final destination might be the same, but the journey feels different. In contexts like these, when aiming for an ambitious fixed target creates too much pressure, setting flexible *open* goals—goals with no specific or measurable end point—can be helpful.

Research on open goals is in its infancy, but their potential to affect how we feel and perform is exciting. In one of the first studies to explore open goals, seventy-eight healthy adults were asked to complete three six-minute walks around the perimeter of a basketball court.[14] After a first walk to record a baseline distance for each person, the study participants were randomly assigned either a specific performance goal (asked to walk 16.67 percent farther during their second walk and 8.33 percent farther during their third), an open performance goal (instructed to see how far they could walk in six minutes during walks two and three), a do-your-best goal (asked to, you guessed it, do their best for six minutes in attempts two and three), or no goal (asked to walk at their normal pace).

Perhaps not surprisingly, the three goal groups walked farther than the no-goal group in walks two and three. But the goal groups didn't differ from each other in total distance walked. There were, however, important differences in terms of how each group felt. Participants given fixed, specific goals reported feeling more pressure to achieve their target during each walk than the other goal groups did. In contrast, having an open goal led to higher interest in repeating the walking session than experienced in any other group. That's an important outcome for people who want to get, and stay, more physically active, because people who are interested in what they're doing are more likely to do it than people who feel like they're "supposed" to do something.

A follow-up study in 2020 found that participants who did not regularly exercise achieved greater six-minute walking distances and reported enjoying the walks more when given an open goal than when given a specific performance goal.[15] In contrast, active individuals—study participants who walked regularly in their everyday lives—achieved greater distances and reported greater enjoyment when they were set a specific goal.

Collectively, these studies suggest that specific goals can make us feel pressured to achieve a fixed standard. This isn't necessarily a bad thing, and this pressure can motivate experienced performers—like the active walkers in the second walking study—to reach higher levels of performance.

But for less experienced individuals, open goals can help to reduce feelings of pressure, increase enjoyment of an activity, and improve performance. This is especially true when we're setting out on the journey to achieve a difficult or ambitious goal, one that might seem beyond our current reach. In those circumstances, focusing on setting an open goal and seeing where it takes us might be a better strategy.

As we'll explore in chapter 3, researchers are also discovering that both specific and open goals can help athletes enter those rare, peak-performance, "in-the-zone" states. Which type of goal works best for athletes—and what we can learn from this—can depend on the context we find ourselves in.

MIND THE GAP

Important though these goal-setting strategies are, chunk-ing, writing goals down, and knowing which type of goal to set are only the beginning of the goal-achievement process. Just because we set a good goal doesn't mean that we'll achieve it. What's more common is that we don't get started or we get derailed en route to our final destination.[16] We fail to mind the gap between setting a goal and following through on it. In the second half of this chapter we'll explore evidence-based strategies that successful athletes use to get started and stay on track to achieve their goals.

IF YOU CAN KEEP YOUR HEAD . . .

The first goal-achievement technique is surprisingly simple but incredibly effective. One reason we often fail to act on our goals is that we make poor choices in certain situations. We delay study plans despite our goal to pass an exam, for exam-ple, or give in to temptations at dessert despite our goal to eat healthier and lose weight. Recognizing these issues, a Ger-man psychology professor, Peter Gollwitzer, developed an elementary tool to help form new responses to challenging situations. He called it *if-then planning*, and formulated it as follows: "*If* situation X arises, *then* I will perform response Y."[17]

The key to if-then planning is that any situation can be linked with a response that's congruent with the goal we're striving to achieve. So instead of merely stating, "I'm going to read this book" or "I want to eat healthier," an if-then plan spells out where, when, or how we will act. These situa-tions—the *if* parts—can be opportunities, such as having quiet time to read and reflect, or obstacles, such as being tempted by junk food.

A great example of planning how to think and act in challenging situations comes from Kansas City Chiefs quarterback Patrick Mahomes. The Chiefs won Super Bowl LIV in 2020 by a score of 31 to 20. What was most impressive was the manner of their victory. Trailing the San Francisco 49ers by 10 points at the end of the third quarter, the Chiefs scored three unanswered touchdowns in the final quarter. Two of these touchdowns resulted from throws by Mahomes, who, by his own admission, hadn't played well to that point.

Written three years before Super Bowl LIV, the following excerpt from Mahomes's NFL draft cover letter in 2017 seems prophetic of his response to the events that unfolded during that game:

> *Football* is under the lights, facing the elements in front of 60,000 people. It's keeping your guys motivated, whatever the circumstances, and having the determination to bring your team back from seemingly certain defeat in the fourth quarter.
>
> It's doing everything you can to make a play in the red zone. Sometimes the play breaks down and you have to get creative.
>
> I'm not perfect. But football isn't always perfect. It doesn't always go the way you expect.[18]

"Whatever the circumstances," such as being behind heading into the final quarter, is the *if* part. Keeping teammates motivated and playing with a determined attitude is the planned *then* response. Focusing on helpful processes like these—as Mahomes had planned he would if he encountered that situation—gives us a much greater chance of achieving our desired outcomes.

Learning from Mahomes's example, we can apply this thinking strategy to our everyday lives. We might plan how we would cope with setbacks or temptations that have the potential to derail our goal-striving attempts. If-then planning has, for example, been shown to be effective in changing eating habits. People with cravings for unhealthy snacks can plan a strategy to cope, such as, "If I think about the unhealthy snack, then I will distract myself and do something else."[19]

But maybe these scenarios are a little too predictable. After all, some goal-striving obstacles are foreseeable. Losing a game heading into the final quarter might be expected, as might the challenge of dealing with cravings. But we can learn from athletes here as well. Planning for less predictable "what-if" moments is something successful athletes do regularly. Often, it involves practicing how they'll think and act—the processes—in response to challenging events. Good planning like this not only helps athletes remain focused and make better decisions; it can also help them avoid panic during unexpected performance disruptions.

One example of planning for "what-if" moments involves American swimmer Michael Phelps, the most successful Olympic athlete of all time and winner of twenty-eight Olympic medals, including twenty-three golds, in his career. Each night, in preparation for races, Phelps would imagine positive and negative scenarios (the *if*) and mentally practice how he would think and respond to cope with each (the *then*). In addition, his coach, Bob Bowman, would create challenges for Phelps during training and less important competitions to practice his *then* responses.

As recounted in Bowman's book *The Golden Rules*, Bowman once deliberately stepped on and cracked Phelps's swimming goggles before a World Cup race in Australia.[20] Phelps didn't notice his goggles were broken until he dived into the pool and they suddenly began to fill with water.

Phelps didn't let the malfunction affect him. Instead, he dealt with the annoyance by counting his strokes, a strategy Bowman and Phelps had developed in training to know exactly how many strokes it took to complete a length of the pool. Intentionally stepping on Phelps's goggles might seem like a pointless exercise, but Bowman believed athletes needed to be prepared to deal with any "what-if" scenario they might encounter in more important competitions. In other words, *if* something unexpected like this happened during a race, *then* remembering to count his strokes would help Phelps to focus on the process of swimming fast and deal with the situation.

Exactly this scenario played out during one of the biggest races of Phelps's career, the 200-meter butterfly final at the 2008 Olympics. In the middle of the race, Phelps's goggles developed a leak and began to fill with water. As a result, he couldn't see the lane markers at the bottom of the pool, the wall at the end of the pool, or where his competitors were. He was, in effect, suddenly swimming in the dark.

Rather than panic, Phelps remained calm. As he had in Australia, he began counting his strokes in the final lap, knowing that it would take twenty-one strokes to swim one length. He increased his pace midway through and reached for the wall after the twenty-first stroke. The result? Another gold medal and a world record.

As the stories of Mahomes and Phelps suggest, if-then plans are particularly effective in helping us overcome challenging obstacles. They help us perform at our best when things go wrong not only in fierce competition but also during everyday events like studying for an exam, making healthier food choices, sticking to an exercise program, or starting a work project. For any of these, most potential difficulties can be countered with an effective plan for how to respond in the best possible way. Right now, you might reflect on adverse events that could derail your goal-striving attempts. Writing these *ifs* down and planning constructive responses can ensure that you stay on the path to achieve your ambition.

The table below provides a structure for doing this. Begin by writing each *if* in the first column. In the second column, write an appropriate *then*—a way you would like to respond to each situation. We've completed two examples to help get you started. The first provides a response to help plan your reading or study activity. The second provides a number of practical, effective solutions to help cope with cravings for unhealthy snacks.

Opportunity/Obstacle (*If...*)	More Helpful Response (*Then...*)
If I have time to myself in the evening . . .	Then I will switch off the TV and read one chapter of my book.
If I think about eating an unhealthy snack...	Then I will drink some water / have some fruit / go for a short walk / brush my teeth instead.

Opportunity/Obstacle (*If...*)	More Helpful Response (*Then...*)

One situation, relevant to both sporting and non-sporting settings, where Noel finds if-then planning useful is during presentations to student or athlete groups. Sometimes he wants to ask these groups a probing question, one that will require everyone in the audience to take time to think carefully before responding. With students, the question might relate to a provocative lecture topic. With athletes, it might be about the thoughts and feelings they experience during difficult performance moments.

Very often, after asking the question, Noel finds himself faced with a wall of silence from the audience. His previous, unhelpful reaction was to immediately fill this pause with "noise." He would suggest various opinions or provide an answer of his own. But these actions weren't congruent with his intentions, which were to encourage students to think for themselves and allow athletes time to reflect on how their thoughts and feelings might influence their reactions during competition. Some time ago, when reviewing his actions, Noel thought about a more appropriate response he could make in this situation. What could he do to give people time to respond to his question without interrupting their silent thinking time? What he came up with was this:

> *If* I ask a question and the room falls silent, *then* I will slowly count to ten in my mind before I speak again.

This strategy helps Noel to stay composed in the moment, despite the unnerving silence in the room. What he typically finds is that he gets to a count of between four and six before someone speaks. Adhering to this plan, however, has meant that he gets more creative and insightful responses because his silence allows each person the time to reflect on his or her experiences. We will explore other strategies for staying focused in the moment in chapter 3.

There's good evidence to support the use of if-then planning to help performance in a range of activities. A 2006 review of ninety-four studies found that people who developed if-then plans had a significantly better goal-achievement rate than those who set goals without if-then planning.[21] The studies covered a range of goals, of the types we aspire to achieve in our day-to-day lives. These included following through on New Year's resolutions, completing health-based self-examinations, recycling, completing written reports at college, and developing a CV.

The key to the success of if-then planning is that we don't need to think on our feet as much when faced with a challenging situation. Our planned responses become more automatic, and as a result, we're more likely to respond in an effective way. If-then plans aren't the same as habits, but they can help us on our way to develop good ones.

MAKE IT A HABIT

Throughout this book, we champion the benefits of thinking like an athlete. When it comes to achieving some of our goals, however, thinking can also be a stumbling block. Or, more accurately, needing to think can be a problem. Let us explain.

When we first try to change a behavior, we have to consciously remind ourselves every time we act. Eating healthier means reminding ourselves to avoid the snacks we normally reach for and choose healthier alternatives instead. Many of the actions we perform each day are habits. Habits, good or bad, are automatic actions, triggered not by our conscious deliberation or planning but instead by cues in our environment. It might be brushing our teeth (habit) after we eat breakfast (trigger), putting a seat belt on (habit) as soon as we sit in a car (trigger), or snacking on junk food (habit) when we watch TV (trigger).

The reason our habits occur with little or no conscious thought is that, after many repetitions, our actions are kick-started by the triggering situation or event. If the habit is a good one, like putting a seat belt on once you enter a car, then great—you don't have to consciously remind yourself every time that you need to put your seat belt on.

But if the habit is an unwanted one, it can be extremely difficult to break. In particular, changing a bad habit requires high levels of motivation and self-control at the outset. Unfortunately, when our levels of motivation and self-control are low, as when we're tired at the end of a long workday, then our habits tend to dominate. This explains why changing old habits and forming new ones can be so difficult.

But this problem also gives us a valuable clue about how to stay on track toward achieving our goals. If we want to change our behaviors permanently, then one solution is to learn how to make good habits that take the place of undesirable ones. What athletes have mastered—and what we can learn from them—is how to rely more on well-developed habits to help them achieve their goals.

A perfect example of this is the calm and composed response of Michael Phelps when his goggles unexpectedly filled with water during the 2008 Olympic butterfly final. Phelps's coach, Bob Bowman, recalls their strategy to prepare for "what-if" moments like that:

> We'd experiment, try different things until we found stuff that worked. Eventually we figured out it was best to concentrate on these tiny moments of success and build them into mental triggers. We worked them into a routine. There's a series of things we do before every race that are designed to give Michael a sense of building victory. If you were to ask Michael what's going on in his head before competition, he would say he's not really thinking about anything. He's just following the program. But that's not right. It's more like his habits have taken over.[22]

So how can we learn to develop good habits like these?

There are four key steps we can take to form new habits.[23] The first two have already been discussed in this chapter. Step one is to set a goal that you would like to achieve. Step two is to decide which actions, or processes, will help you achieve your goal. An important point with habit formation, however, is that it's easier to develop habits consisting of relatively simple behaviors than it is to develop habits involving more complex ones. Brushing your teeth or putting a seat belt on, for example, involves a small number of steps and, therefore, can become a strong habit relatively quickly. But more complex behaviors, like exercising, are more challenging because there are many actions involved. To go for a walk or run, you must choose what to wear, put your workout clothes on, lace up your shoes, decide where to go, and then leave your house. Once you get started on that sequence, however, you're more likely to follow the steps that, ultimately, result in starting to exercise.

The key to habit formation, then, even for more complex behaviors, is to focus on the first critical steps of the sequence.[24] This is where if-then planning can help you get started. *If* you want to seize an opportunity to exercise before breakfast, for example, *then* you might set your clothes and shoes out at bedtime the previous evening so that these are the first things you see after getting out of bed. In this way, getting out of bed and seeing your clothes becomes the trigger that gets the sequence started. To avoid getting derailed, you might also make a coping plan for potential hazards that could trip you up along the way, such as, "*If* I don't feel like exercising after I lace up my shoes, *then* I will step outside before I make a final decision." Once you leave your house, you're more likely to continue your exercise plans. Combining this with an open goal to see how far you can go can also help if you're starting to exercise for the first time.

The third and fourth steps are closely related to each other, but both are essential to form new habits. First, as you might imagine, you have to practice and repeat the new behavior regularly. But what helps to make this new behavior a habit—the fourth step—is to repeat it consistently in the same context and in response to the same trigger. This is what Michael Phelps did to develop good habit responses to challenging events. By repeatedly practicing your response, you create a mental association between the trigger and the behavior that follows. In fact, studies have shown that simply being reminded of a trigger is enough to bring thoughts of an activity to mind.[25] In this way, as Bob Bowman suggested, habits take over. With practice and repetition, our actions become less reliant on conscious thoughts, and are driven instead by our automatic responses to triggers around us.

A similar approach can also be taken to breaking unwanted or "bad" habits. First, the fact that habits are triggered by cues around you means that one way of breaking an old habit is to identify and reduce your exposure to whatever triggers it in the first place. As an example, making healthier food choices might begin with buying fewer unhealthy snacks. In turn, buying fewer snacks might mean you avoid walking down the snack aisle (trigger) when shopping in the grocery store.

But avoiding habit triggers isn't always possible. In these contexts, other strategies can help. When you're exposed to a trigger, repeating a simple instruction to yourself, like "Don't do it," can help override your usual habit response.[26] As we saw with if-then planning, replacing the old habit with a new action can also help you cope with triggering events. In this way, breaking a habit becomes less about stopping an old behavior and more about forming a new association between a trigger and how you respond to it.

Finally, it's worth reminding yourself that forming new habits can take time. To study the process of habit formation, researchers at University College London asked ninety-six students to choose one healthy behavior that they would like to make into a once-daily habit.[27] The choices they were given included eating a piece of fruit or drinking a bottle of water with lunch, exercising by running for fifteen minutes before dinner, and going for a walk after breakfast. Over the course of twelve weeks, the students were required to track their behavior daily and also complete a questionnaire that measured how automatic—or habitual—the new behavior felt.

The results suggested that it took, on average, sixty-six days for the new healthy behaviors to become automatic. But there was a lot of individual variation. Simpler behaviors, like drinking water with lunch, became habits much quicker than more complex ones, like exercising, did. Deeper analysis of the data also suggested that it took anywhere between 18 and 254 days for some individuals to make the new behaviors automatic. In other words, it can take many weeks and even months to develop new habits. What helps, however, is knowing the steps you can apply to help you on your way.

A FINAL WORD ON GOALS

Achieving our ambitions, no matter how small or big, often means learning how to focus on the process—attending to the step-by-step actions that help us reach a performance or outcome goal. Planning how we would like to act and using habit-formation strategies are important tools to have in our kit.

As we've seen with the examples of Patrick Mahomes and Michael Phelps, however, habits don't involve only our actions. We can make our thoughts and emotional responses to challenging events a habit, too. These responses include staying calm and composed when things aren't going to plan. In the next chapter, we'll explore emotional responses to triggering events and discover how thinking like an athlete can help us manage how we feel and act under even the most difficult of circumstances.

CHAPTER 2

There Is Nothing Either Good or Bad

The Emotion-Regulation Tools

———

IN INTERNATIONAL MEN'S RUGBY UNION, no team quite compares with the New Zealand All Blacks. Since their first game in 1903, their 77.3 winning percentage remains unparalleled, with only South Africa, at 65 percent, coming close.[1] In 2015, the All Blacks, captained by Richie McCaw, the "G.A.B." we met in chapter 1, became the first team to win three Rugby World Cups. (World Cups are held once every four years.) In 2013, they became the first, and still only, international team to win all of their games in a calendar year. In fact, in the four years between the start of the 2011 Rugby World Cup and the end of the 2015 tournament—both of which they won—they were victorious in a staggering 92 percent of their sixty-one games.

But it wasn't always this way. Before their 2011 tournament win, New Zealand's record at the Rugby World Cup was less impressive. Since claiming the inaugural title in 1987, the All Blacks had routinely fallen short of expectations as favorites in subsequent tournaments. They lost at the semifinal stage in 1991, 1999, and 2003, and lost to South Africa in the final in 1995.

Their lowest moment came in the 2007 tournament, when they lost 18–20 to France in the quarterfinals, New Zealand's worst-ever outcome at a Rugby World Cup. It was a tournament the All Blacks were—as in most Rugby World Cups—the overwhelming favorites to win. They had won thirty-four of their thirty-nine games before the tournament. Those games included a 61–10 win against France in Wellington, New Zealand, just four months before the quarterfinal game, and a 47–3 win in Lyon, France, just eleven months earlier, France's heaviest-ever "home" defeat. So confident were New Zealanders that they would win the quarterfinal game that the country's leading newspaper, the *New Zealand Herald*, headlined their game preview, FRANCE POSE ABSOLUTELY NO THREAT TO THE ALL BLACKS, and boasted, "The All Blacks could play in sackcloths and they'd still stomp all over France."[2]

Amid much soul-searching during their post-tournament review, the All Blacks' head coach, Graham Henry, and his assistants recognized two key factors in their defeat: a collective failure to make good decisions under pressure and an inability to manage their emotions when it really mattered. The final eleven minutes of play during their defeat against France supports this conclusion; it makes for uncomfortable viewing if you're a New Zealand supporter. Having fallen behind to an ultimately decisive French score in the sixty-ninth minute, the All Blacks committed a litany of errors during the panic-stricken moments that ensued.

After their defeat, the New Zealand players and coaches were criticized for errors in decision-making and skill execution that resulted in six lost possessions in those frantic final minutes. For the number-one-ranked team in the world, that was unthinkable. In short, with the game on the line and when composure was critical, the All Blacks choked.

In a sporting context, choking occurs when a skilled athlete suddenly experiences a dramatic dip in performance under pressure.[3] You can probably recall other occasions in sport where the overwhelming favorite catastrophically underperformed when it mattered most. It's not uncommon, and it doesn't happen just in sport. Performing poorly in an exam or stumbling through a presentation can be the result of pressure-induced choking, too. Most of us have experienced what pressure can do and the impact it can have on our performance. But few of us know what we can do about it. How can we learn to perform under pressure as effectively as successful athletes do?

In this chapter, we'll answer that question and explore some of the key strategies that athletes have learned to help them cope in contexts like these. To appreciate how our performance can suffer, we first need to understand what happens when we experience a pressurized situation.

SIGNS OF STRESS

When we encounter a situation that we perceive as threatening or dangerous, our body undergoes an immediate stress response. It begins in a region of the brain called the amygdala and involves a rapid sequence of events that leads to a number of physiological reactions: an accelerated heart rate, faster breathing, tense muscles, and sweaty palms. If you've ever felt nervous, you know what these reactions feel like.

Termed *fight-or-flight*, this innate reaction to stress evolved over millions of years to energize and protect us in situations where our safety is at risk. It's triggered almost instantly by emotions like anxiety and fear. You might imagine how quickly you would react if an angry dog started to chase you. In a situation like this, the physiological changes you experience enhance your physical strength (to help you fight a potential threat) and increase your speed and stamina (to propel you to safety).

In our modern lives, we frequently face situations that we perceive as threatening or dangerous in some way. Instead of the physical threats—like hungry predators—that our ancestors might have encountered, our modern threats are mostly psychological in nature. In an important sporting contest, an academic exam, or a public speech, we risk feeling embarrassed, worry that we'll let ourselves or others down, or dread that we'll be judged negatively by an audience. These outcome-focused thoughts create the pressure under which we attempt to perform. And this is where our natural stress response can start to cause problems.

Perceived psychological threats, and a sense that we may not have the tools to cope, trigger not only a fight-or-flight stress response but also increased angst about the implications of performing poorly. In such a state, with our focus on anything but the process at hand, we will, almost inevitably, perform poorly. We might forget our game plan, what we studied before the exam, or what we wanted to say to our audience. In some cases, we also experience a third component of our stress response: We freeze. Different from fight-or-flight, freezing causes us to remain rooted to the spot, disconnected from the world around us and unable to take decisive action, like a deer caught in the headlights.

What these examples demonstrate is that it's often not the situation that's the issue. After all, athletes perform successfully during once-in-a-lifetime events, students excel during exams, and history is replete with examples of outstanding public orations. Instead, it's the thoughts we have and emotions we experience that often prove problematic.

But if we accept this premise, then we also unlock the key to performing better under pressure. Because if our thoughts and emotional responses are the problem, then learning to control our thoughts, manage our emotions, and think like a successful athlete under pressure is the solution. This was precisely the conclusion that the All Blacks reached following their 2007 Rugby World Cup exit.

AN EMOTIONAL FRAMEWORK

In their attempt to understand why the team failed to perform during their 2007 defeat by France, the All Black coaching staff, along with forensic psychiatrist Ceri Evans, developed a simple metaphor to describe the emotional state they experienced during that game. They called it "red."[4]

Evans conceptualized some of our brain functions as a "red" system. The red system includes many of the things that our brain takes care of without our conscious awareness. These include physiological processes such as heart rate, breathing, and sweating. Think of the red system as our autopilot, taking care of the bodily functions that keep us alive.

Most of the time, operations run smoothly. But the red system is constantly on alert and has evolved lightning-quick reactions if anything threatens our safety. These instantaneous reactions include our stress response. In situations where a threat is detected, red's priority is to prime us for swift action.

This all sounds fine so far. Being primed to act swiftly is a good thing. But again, this fight-or-flight response evolved in a world of physical danger, whereas many of our dangers—our threats—are psychological. And when we experience intense emotions like fear or anxiety under psychological pressure, our innate stress responses can hijack our performance. When we experience a strong stress response, we act on instinct, and our ability to think clearly and logically is compromised. Instead, we become focused on the sources of threat we perceive. An athlete gets distracted by the game clock ticking down, the reactions of the crowd, and the consequences of losing. She might also become self-focused, meaning that she pays too much attention to her own actions, intent on executing them perfectly rather than letting them happen naturally. (If you've ever tripped on a staircase when others were watching you, you know what we're talking about.) As a result, we make poor decisions and commit errors in our basic skills that lead to worse performance. Each of these threat reactions were evidenced in the New Zealand players during those final minutes of their 2007 Rugby World Cup campaign.

Evans conceptualized other brain functions as a "blue" system. These include our abilities to think rationally and logically, to solve problems, to plan a course of action, and to be aware of our own mental states. Largely governed by the frontal lobes of our brain, "blue" provides a much slower, more deliberate, and more reasoned response to demanding events. These brain systems allow us to maintain control over our emotional responses and provide a task-relevant focus that's critical to performing well under pressure. In a nutshell, blue's priority is to think clearly.

But there's the rub. To perform well under psychological pressure, we must combine our actions with thinking. We need to coordinate our fast-acting red system and our slower-thinking blue system to get the best of both. In other words, controlling our thoughts and emotional responses under pressure—staying calm and focused—means using the mental tools that successful athletes have learned. And unless we know what they are, and how to use them, performing under pressure is almost impossible.

What you might have begun to realize is that neither of these systems is good or bad. Our innate stress response can save our life, but too much red and we react in hot-headed, instinctual ways that are unlikely to be successful under pressure. Equally, logic and reasoning help us solve problems, but too much blue during performance means we overthink and lack the drive to act decisively. What's important is being able to recognize and understand which state we are in and adjust our mental thermostat so that our red/blue balance is just right.

We can think about most of our emotional responses in the same way as our red and blue systems. Although we might think of sadness, anxiety, or anger as only bad, these unpleasant emotions can be useful.[5] Feeling some worry about an upcoming exam can drive a student to study diligently, for example. In this way, feeling pre-performance concern can be helpful.

Equally, we might consider excitement and contentment as inherently good emotions. They certainly feel pleasant. But as we learned in chapter 1, feeling contented with our progress on a task can lead us to become complacent and fall short of achieving a goal. If this happens, then our feelings of contentment were, ultimately, unhelpful.

Therefore, rather than being good or bad, emotions are better thought of as pleasant or unpleasant, and helpful or unhelpful. Managing our emotions, then, has two key payoffs. We do it to feel better, and/or we do it to perform better.

Knowing how our brain responds to stress is a good starting point to learn how to manage our emotions and perform better under pressure. Knowing that the emotions we experience are neither good nor bad is also useful. A next step is to become more aware of the emotions we experience in any situation. Once we can recognize our emotions, and label them appropriately, we're well on our way to the final step of being able to manage these emotional responses more easily.

WHAT EMOTION AM I FEELING?

How do you feel right now? Maybe you've had a tough day and you're feeling slightly tense or annoyed. Maybe you're feeling calm and relaxed as you read this book. Or maybe it would be more accurate to say you're feeling calmer since you began to read this book. If so, great—and not just because it means you're enjoying this book. It shines a spotlight on one of the critical features of our emotions: They're malleable. When we need to, we can do something to change them.

We experience many different emotions daily, and these can be the result of events that happen, thoughts that we have, or memories that we reflect on. However we feel, central to all emotions are two basic feeling states.[6] The first— just like our stress response—involves feeling high or low levels of energy. You can recognize a high-energy state by noticing when your heart beats faster, your breathing rate quickens, your muscles tense, your body temperature rises, or you feel more alert.

The second dimension involves emotions that feel either pleasant or unpleasant. Together, these two dimensions, and some examples of the emotions we experience, can be represented in four quadrants, as shown in the diagram below.[7]

Excitement, for example, is a pleasant, high-energy state and is located in the top-right quadrant alongside elation and delight. Anger and anxiety are high-energy but unpleasant states and are found in the top-left quadrant alongside frustration. Sadness, depression, and boredom are unpleasant, low-energy states (bottom left), whereas calmness, relaxation, and contentment are low-energy but pleasant states (bottom right). As you read this, you might place other emotions that come to mind in any one of these four quadrants.

Our Basic Feeling States and Some of Our Emotions

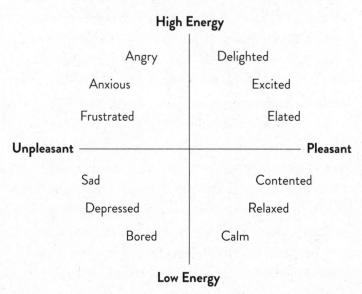

Here's why it's useful to know this: The aim of an emotion-regulation strategy is to change these basic feeling states by shifting us from one quadrant to another. Anxiety, anger, or excitement might require us to calm down by lowering our activation level. In contrast, feeling bored, sad, or depressed might mean we do something, like speak with someone or go for a run, to feel better or more energized.[8]

In this way, being able to recognize our emotions is a crucial step in changing how we feel. You can start this process in any situation by taking a moment to ask yourself what emotion you're feeling and giving it a name. Naming an emotion, as by saying, "I feel angry" or "I feel anxious," is in itself an emotion-regulation strategy and can dampen the intensity of strong emotions by activating our logical "blue" brain.[9]

Other strategies can help too. Managing our emotions means having the right mental tools at our disposal. Without these skills, as many of us have experienced, our emotions can get the better of us. So, what have athletes learned, and how can we take advantage of their insights, to regulate our own emotions when we need to do so?

HOW CAN I REGULATE MY EMOTIONS?

There are more than 160 distinct strategies we can choose from to change how we feel.[10] Most of us use some of them every day. Some strategies involve doing something, like going shopping, listening to music, exercising, or seeking support from a friend. Others involve thinking something, or changing how we're thinking, as by switching off, daydreaming, or thinking rationally about a problem.

Some strategies, like daydreaming, help us avoid unpleasant feelings. Others, like thinking rationally about a problem, are focused on engaging with our emotions and addressing the causes of them. Both sets of strategies can be useful, depending on the context. Sometimes it can be better to distract ourselves, especially when there's little we can do to change a situation. When we have more control over the trigger of our emotions, it might be better to problem-solve and do something productive.

Athletes have learned to use many different approaches to regulate their emotions. Runners, for example, have been found to use any of twenty-eight different strategies in the hour before a race, in the hope of feeling better or performing at their best.[11] These strategies include focusing on their goals, distracting themselves, repeating motivational statements, and recalling past performance successes.

The figures in the previous three paragraphs look like good news. They show us that there are lots of different strategies to help change how we feel. But, like the New Zealand All Blacks in 2007, we don't always know the right tools to use. We need to learn them. And with so many options to choose from, there's a flip side, in that we sometimes get it wrong. Not all emotion-regulation strategies are healthy or even helpful. Behaviors like drinking alcohol or taking drugs might change our feelings in the short term, but the longer-term consequences are often harmful. Similarly, ruminating by focusing on negative thoughts, emotions, and their causes and venting our emotions—by screaming or breaking things—are unhelpful and are associated with poorer mental health and an increase in aggressive feelings, respectively.[12]

Suppressing emotions—attempting to hide our feelings after we've experienced them—can also prove futile. Suppression requires self-control, and our ability to maintain self-control weakens over time, meaning we might eventually feel unpleasant emotions more intensely, or vent them more volatilely.

You might think that athletes are the masters of emotion suppression. After all, some exude a sense of calm under intense pressure. But many athletes have learned that suppressing unhelpful emotions isn't the best way to do this. Their case is strengthened by the findings of a stomach-churning study that explored the effects of emotion suppression on sports performance.[13] For this investigation, the researchers recruited twenty competitive student-athletes and asked them to complete three 10-kilometer cycling time trials in a random sequence. One of the time trials involved no special features. Participants simply came to the lab and completed the 10-kilometer ride as quickly as possible. Before the other two time trials, however, participants viewed a three-minute video that showed a woman causing herself to throw up and, afterward (look away now), eat her own vomit! The thought of this probably makes you feel intense disgust. We can only imagine how it must have felt for the study participants who viewed it.

But this was the key part of the study. As disgusted as they might feel, in one of the time trials, participants were asked to do everything they could to suppress their emotion during and after watching the video. In the other trial, they were able to express their feelings as they wished.

The results revealed that participants completed the suppression time trial an average of twenty-five seconds, or 2.3

percent, slower than they completed the non-suppression time trial, and thirty-six seconds, or 3.4 percent, slower than the no-video trial. Despite this slower speed, they reported that the suppression trial felt *harder* than both of the other trials.

What this study suggests is that emotion suppression, and the self-control and mental effort required to do it, comes at a cost. Suppressing unpleasant emotions, like disgust, anxiety, or anger, not only harms athletic performance. Doing so can detract from other areas of our lives. It can, for example, increase the longer-term likelihood of conflicts, poor relationships, and substance abuse.[14] Having healthier ways of expressing or managing our emotions, just like athletes have learned to do, is important to both our performance and our long-term health and well-being.

So which strategies can help? Which strategies have athletes learned to use to perform better under pressure? In the second half of this chapter, we'll learn about some of the most effective tools we can use to regulate our emotions. We'll begin with reappraisal, and explore how changing the meaning we attach to a situation can modify the emotions we subsequently experience.

THINK AGAIN

In the words of Hamlet, "There is nothing either good or bad, but thinking makes it so." We've already learned that emotions are neither good nor bad, but what about our thinking? How can it "make it so"? When we appraise an event, we judge whether it will help or hinder our pursuit of an important goal. This appraisal can trigger emotions like frustration, anxiety, contentment, or elation, depending on how well we think we're progressing.

Here's an example. If someone offers you some cake because it's your birthday, you might think, "How thoughtful, they remembered it's my birthday." Determined to enjoy your celebration, you might feel content as you sample a mouthful. If, on a separate day, someone offers you some cake, but you're trying to eat healthier, you might think, "How thoughtless, they forgot about my healthier eating plans." You might feel annoyed as you push it aside, or resentful as you politely eat something you'd prefer not to.

In sporting contexts, falling behind late in a game—as the New Zealand All Blacks did against France in the 2007 Rugby World Cup quarterfinal—is likely to be appraised negatively. But not always. As mentioned in chapter 1, Patrick Mahomes and the Kansas City Chiefs demonstrated during the final quarter of Super Bowl LIV that events not going the way one might hope is an opportunity to act with determination and perform creatively. As Hamlet reasoned, situations by themselves are neither good nor bad. What we think in response to those situations—our appraisals—can make them so.

The principle of *re*-appraisal stems from understanding how events can influence our thoughts, how our thoughts can influence our emotions, and how both our thoughts and our emotions can influence how we act. By changing what we think about an event, we can alter the trajectory of our emotional responses to that event. This strategy—thinking differently—has a powerful impact on our brain. Neuroimaging studies have shown that when we reappraise potentially upsetting information, areas of the brain associated with strong emotional responses, such as the amygdala (our "red" system center), are less activated. At the same time, regions of the brain associated with logical thinking, such as the prefrontal cortex (part of our "blue" system), become more active.[15] In other words, reappraisal helps us strike a better balance between these two states.

Let's put the reappraisal tool into action. To do so, we'll use the example of a field hockey player about to play an important game in front of a big crowd for the first time.[16] Her negative appraisals of that situation might be, "I bet I make mistakes in front of all those people" or "I don't think I can do this." In turn, these thoughts might make her feel worried, anxious, or even scared.

These types of thoughts are normal, and most of us experience them. But let's run through her options for how she can deal with them.[17] First, there's little she can do to change the situation, such as the importance of the game or the actions of the audience. She could decide not to turn up or play, but that isn't going to be helpful. But changing her thoughts to more helpful ones can change the emotions she subsequently feels.

So, to counter her initial negative thoughts, she might instead think, "The crowd makes no difference to how well I can play," or "I have prepared well and earned the right to play in this game." With these reappraisals, she's still likely to feel some pre-competition anxiety, and that's OK. But it's likely to be less intense than the response her initial appraisals would have led to.

We can apply the reappraisal technique in many other ways. Reappraisal can involve putting your problems into perspective, making the best of circumstances, or reminding yourself that, no matter how difficult or prolonged a challenging situation seems, it too will pass.

This process isn't as easy as we've set out here. Learning how to change your initial negative thoughts takes practice and persistence. It begins with becoming more aware of what you automatically say to yourself in difficult or pressurized situations and, in turn, understanding how those thoughts influence how you feel. Writing down the situation, your thoughts, and the resulting emotions can help you recognize triggers and increase your awareness of how you respond to these events.

To help you on this journey, we've included a reappraisal table to structure this activity. You can use the first three columns to write about your thoughts and emotions in response to various situations or events.

Once you become more aware of how you typically think in a situation, and how these thoughts make you feel, the next step is to develop alternative thoughts that you might say to yourself in the same situation. It's important that these new thoughts are likely to bring about a more helpful emotional response. For this, writing down how these alternative thoughts might make you feel is useful. The final two columns of the table provide space for you to write down these alternative thoughts and potential emotional consequences.

Intriguingly, we can also use reappraisal to change unhelpful or unpleasant emotions once we experience them. When we get anxious, for example, the physical reactions we experience—such as a racing heart or sweaty palms—can intensify unhelpful worry and a sense of dread. But reappraising these physical responses as a sign that our body is getting ready to perform at its best can help.[18]

Reappraisal Table

Situation Describe a past situation or event.	Automatic Thoughts What did you think at the time?	Emotions What did you feel at the time?	Alternative Thoughts What more helpful thoughts might you have instead?	Emotions How might those new thoughts make you feel!?

Reappraising their physical sensations, and interpreting them as feelings that can help performance, is something many athletes have learned to do. A great example comes from New England Patriots placekicker Stephen Gostkowski ahead of Super Bowl LIII in 2019. On being asked how he handles pregame nerves, Gostkowski responded:

> Being nervous before a game is a good thing. Not having any emotion at all, to me, is the thing you have to worry about. If you have to get yourself geared up to play this game, something's wrong with you. It's just one of those things. It's a good nervous. It's an excited nervous.[19]

But this strategy doesn't just help athletes in sporting competition. It can also help us in our everyday lives. Simply repeating straightforward statements out loud—for example, saying, "I am excited," when feeling anxious—can help us feel more confident and perform better in a range of tasks, including solving math problems under pressure and speaking in public.[20] In other words, interpreting feelings of anxiety as something that can help, rather than hinder, our performance can have a positive impact on how we ultimately perform.

Reappraisal of anxiety as excitement involves a left-to-right, unpleasant-to-pleasant shift in our basic feeling states. For athletes, this can help to maintain the energizing benefits of higher activation while negating the unhelpful impact of anxiety and worry.

WRITE ABOUT IT

We've already learned about the dangers of suppressing our emotions. There are more helpful strategies to help manage our emotional state. One of these is journaling, a tool to help us express, rather than suppress, our thoughts, feelings, and insights. Journaling has been shown to lower distress and depression, enhance psychological well-being, and improve physical health. This is especially true when we try to make sense of a situation and deal with it constructively as we write about it.[21]

Writing about how we feel can help to regulate our emotions in many ways.[22] Writing can act as a form of emotion labeling, for example, the "what emotion am I feeling?" strategy we presented earlier. When we attach words to our feelings, it helps to change how we process our emotional responses.

Expressive writing is helpful in many situations. Although difficult and upsetting, writing about the thoughts and emotions associated with traumatic life events, such as parental divorce, the experience of racial prejudice, or the death of a loved one, has been shown to increase our sense of personal growth and self-acceptance and decrease feelings of distress. Writing about a traumatic experience, and developing a greater insight into the event, can also increase our sense of personal resilience, meaning that we feel more optimistic and have greater control of the event and our emotions.[23]

These beneficial effects of expressive writing may explain why many athletes regularly keep a journal. Serena Williams, the twenty-three-time Grand Slam tennis champion, has suggested that writing down one's thoughts and feelings in a notebook "can help clear out negative thoughts and emotions that keep you feeling stuck."[24] Two-time Olympic champion Alpine skier Mikaela Shiffrin has kept a journal since she was thirteen. In it, she records her thoughts and feelings about the positive and negative events that occur daily in her athletic and non-athletic worlds.[25]

A second way we can use a journal is to practice expressing gratitude for the positive things in our life, no matter what the source. This can include writing about things that our family, friends, or colleagues have given us or done for us, or even the difficulties and challenges we've come through.

Focusing on gratitude can help us to view situations more positively and change the emotions we subsequently experience. One study found that individuals who maintained a gratitude journal for four weeks were more effective at reappraising unpleasant images and, consequently, at regulating their emotional responses to them than a group who didn't practice expressing gratitude.[26]

The personal growth that can be achieved by keeping a gratitude journal is evident in the story of six-time Olympic sprint champion Allyson Felix.[27] Felix, who writes in a gratitude journal daily, reflected in an interview in early 2020:

> I think the place I'm in now is just appreciative for the experiences. My younger self couldn't handle that. But now I'm grateful for the hard moments. . . . It's taught me a lot about myself. I've grown a lot; I've definitely been tested. It's almost like this is where I want to be going into those final years, where I'm confident but still hungry and very secure in who I am.[28]

Specific to anxiety, one final way we can use journaling is to engage in worry time. As counterintuitive as it sounds, spending time deliberately focusing on our worries—in a constructive way—can help to reduce feelings of anxiety.[29]

In other words, worrying on purpose can help us worry less. Writing about our worries can increase our sense of control over things we might worry about and, in turn, focus our mind on solutions to those issues. Worry time also means we avoid the negative consequences of trying to suppress how we're feeling.

Worry time involves five steps.[30] First, schedule a period of time, say twenty minutes, with no distractions to interrupt you. Plan this as a time when you can worry on purpose. Second, during this time, write down a list of all the things you're worried about. Don't attempt to stop any worries at this point. No matter how major or trivial they might seem, write them down.

Once you've got them all written, the third step is to give each worry a rating of 1, 2, or 3. The 1s are worries you can act on and do something about. The 2s are worries you may be able to do something about, and the 3s are worries you can do nothing about. These 3s might be situations or events that are completely outside your control.

Fourth, problem-solve for each worry, beginning with the 1s, then the 2s, and finally the 3s. Be specific with these solutions and think of them as future actions that you'll develop goals for (see chapter 1). You might set a specific time to act on a solution to your most pressing worry, for example.

It's likely you'll discover there's nothing you can do about some worries, like some 2s and all 3s. That's OK—accepting that there are some things you can't change can lead to more helpful emotional responses. Attempting to reappraise these situations might also be helpful to ease these concerns.

Once worry time is over, the final step is to put these thoughts aside for the rest of the day, unless you're acting on one of your worry solutions. It's inevitable that you'll start to think of your worries outside of worry time, especially when you first start to schedule worry time. But this is OK! Reminding yourself that you'll return to those worries during worry time the next day can help to manage these thoughts.

Other strategies, such as distraction (like going for a walk or having a conversation about something completely different), can change your focus of attention outside of worry time. We'll cover these strategies in chapter 3. Scheduling time to focus on relaxation techniques—like those that follow—can also help to release tension and manage unpleasant emotional responses.

BREATHE AND RELAX

So, you've practiced reappraisal, and you've written about your feelings. Both have helped. But now you're sitting in the waiting room about to enter a job interview and you're feeling edgier than you would like. What can you do?

This is the same question athletes face. What can they do in the heat of the moment to stay calm and composed?

Learning the mental techniques needed to calm down quickly was a core strategy in the All Blacks' post-2007 red--to-blue switch. Calming down requires changing a strong emotional response, such as frustration, anxiety, or anger, to a lower arousal state. The strategies below will allow you to regulate your emotions after you've experienced an intense emotional response.

One of the most effective ways of calming down in the moment is centering. Centering is a breathing technique that involves taking a slow, deep breath by filling your lungs fully and pushing your stomach out as you breathe in. As you momentarily hold your breath, also focus on any tension you might feel anywhere in your body, such as your back, shoulders, or face. Finally, as you slowly and completely exhale, focus on relaxing your muscles and releasing tension at the same time. The entire process can take as little as a few seconds.

Many athletes take slow, deep breaths to ready themselves as part of a pre-performance routine. Soccer players like Megan Rapinoe and Cristiano Ronaldo use deep breaths to calm down before striking a free kick. Biathletes like Dorothea Wierer and Johannes Thingnes Boe use breathing techniques to lower their heart rate and reduce tension during the transition from cross-country skiing to target shooting. In research studies, pre-performance deep breaths have been shown to improve youth basketballers' free-throw shooting performance[31] and, when combined with instructional and positive self-talk, improve the save percentage of ice hockey goaltenders.[32]

The Girls on the Run program that we introduced at the start of the book includes a tool called Stop and Take a BrThRR, which applies these skills to other life domains. This strategy teaches girls to stop, breathe, think, respond, and review to manage their emotions and respond more constructively in difficult situations. Feedback from girls who completed the program suggests that Stop and Take a BrThRR was most useful in managing emotions like annoyance, anger, and frustration when they were being teased or during a disagreement with a sibling, for example.[33]

There are other relaxation techniques you can use if you have a little more time. One of the most effective is progressive muscular relaxation, or PMR. Originally developed in the 1930s, PMR involves sequentially tensing and relaxing the muscles of the body, beginning with your hands and arms and continuing until you reach your feet and toes. The purpose of PMR is to help you develop a greater awareness of muscle tension and, when you notice it, release that tension and relax.

We've included a sample PMR script in appendix 2 to help you begin. The complete routine takes approximately twenty minutes. We recommend you give it a go when you have time to practice relaxation, such as just before you go to sleep. Once you learn the technique, a shorter version is helpful in the hours before an important event—or while you sit in a waiting room—to manage your emotional state.

In everyday life, PMR is effective for situations where tension and anxiety are problematic. You can use PMR to manage work-related stress, reduce insomnia, or relieve tension headaches.[34] When used as part of cognitive behavioral therapy, PMR has been shown to help treat generalized anxiety disorders, panic disorders, social phobia, and chronic pain, and to reduce psychological distress in cancer patients.[35]

It's also good to know that you can use these tools in combination. Deep breathing coupled with reappraisal can help you achieve the twin aims of relaxing and changing your thoughts in stressful situations. The All Blacks' red-to-blue strategy began with slow, deep breaths to calm players down during pressurized moments. Next, players used an individualized grounding technique to refocus their attention back into the present moment.

KEEP YOUR FEET ON THE GROUND

When we experience a strong emotion, we focus excessively on thoughts related to that emotion. When we get angry, we ruminate over the source of our rage, for example. As we learned earlier in this chapter, when athletes get anxious, they get distracted by their own worries and fears or pay too much attention to a skill they normally execute automatically. These anxiety-induced changes in attention are a root cause of choking and otherwise performing worse. The final tool in this chapter is a deceptively simple procedure you can use to alter this sequence of events.

Grounding techniques help to break this chain of events and focus your mind back into the present moment. Listening to music, exercising, deep breathing, and reading a book are all examples of grounding techniques.

One of the most common versions of grounding, known as the 5-4-3-2-1 technique, involves each of our five external senses. You can practice this right now. Scan your surroundings and, either out loud or silently, slowly list five things you can see, four things you can feel or touch, three things you can hear, two things you can smell, and one thing you can taste. Don't stop until you have found all fifteen items.

If you were fully engaged in mentally searching for these items, you are now more aware of some sensations that you hadn't paid much attention to until that point. You might notice the feeling of your back against the chair or, perhaps, the smell of the pages of the book in your hand. This is the purpose of grounding—to focus your attention on the present moment and away from distracting or unhelpful thoughts. You may not notice a big difference in your emotional state right now; hopefully you were already feeling calm and relaxed. But grounding when you're anxious, angry, or frustrated can help to lower the intensity of these feelings and manage your emotional state.

Scott benefited from this technique almost immediately after Noel taught it to him. About ninety minutes into a four-hour training run (don't ask), Scott was struggling mentally. His usual strategies, such as chunking the remaining time and reminding himself that the run was a building block to a personally meaningful goal, weren't working. Scott remained hung up on, "I don't feel like doing this. I'm not even halfway, and then I'll still have another two hours to go. Too much of my life is spent waiting things out rather than enjoying myself." He started rationalizing why it would be OK to cut the run significantly short, even though he felt fine physically.

Then he recalled the 5-4-3-2-1 technique and went through the five-senses checklist. Still feeling distracted by woe-is-me thoughts, he did the exercise again, but with a condition: He couldn't include any of the things he'd seen, heard, etc., the first time around. Coming up with separate taste sensations after running several miles is difficult! By the time Scott completed his second cycle through the exercise, he'd been running for close to two hours. His thinking shifted to more helpful lines, such as, "You're almost halfway done, and now you're heading toward your favorite stretch of forest." The rest of the run passed uneventfully, and Scott met his goal for the day.

Being able to regulate your emotions quickly is important in many performance contexts. In scenarios like these, you probably won't have time to complete the full 5-4-3-2-1 grounding exercise (much less do it twice!). But practicing and refining a short grounding strategy based on your individual needs can be useful.

So, how can you put it all together? How can you use breathing and grounding to manage your emotions when you're starting to feel the pressure?

This is exactly what members of the post-2007 All Blacks team learned to do. One player, Kieran Read, would ground himself by scanning the stadium to focus his attention externally on the bigger picture. Using a different sensory channel, his teammate Richie McCaw would sometimes stamp his boot in the ground during brief breaks in play and focus on the feeling in his foot. McCaw described how he put the deep-breathing and grounding techniques together in his autobiography, *The Real McCaw*:

> Breathing slowly and deliberately, nose or mouth, with a two-second pause. While breathing, hold your wrist on the out-breath. Then shift your attention to something external—the ground or your feet, or the ball in hand, or even alternating big toes, or the grandstand. Get your eyes up, looking out.
>
> You've got to use deep breaths and key words to help yourself get out of your own head, find an external focus, get yourself back in the present, regain your situational awareness.[36]

For the All Blacks, perfecting these strategies certainly seemed to work. Four years after their defeat to France in the 2007 tournament, New Zealand faced the same opponents in the 2011 final. In a tight, tense battle, equal to the 2007 encounter, the All Blacks edged a 1-point victory, 8–7, to win their first Rugby World Cup title in twenty-four years. Four years later, in the 2015 tournament, they became the first team to retain the title, beating Australia 34–17 in the final.

A FINAL WORD ON EMOTION REGULATION

There are many strategies that you can use to regulate your emotions. But managing emotions can be difficult, and choosing the right strategy isn't always easy. Being more aware of the emotions you experience, and having a range of helpful tools at your disposal, is important. But learning these techniques and using them effectively can take practice and patience. Don't expect them to work instantly. Instead, try many over time to find out which work best for you.

As the 5-4-3-2-1 grounding technique demonstrates, being able to focus or refocus your attention can also help to regulate your emotions. But there are other techniques you can use to manage your concentration. We'll turn to those strategies in the next chapter.

CHAPTER 3

What Were You Thinking?

The Focus and Concentration Tools

———

IF YOU'LL INDULGE US for a moment, we'd like to tell you a personal story that's relevant to this chapter.

In 2006, Scott went to India to cover a five-day stage race in the Himalayan foothills. The day before the race, he and the eventual winner went for a run from the race headquarters in Mirik. There was a small lake with a perimeter path nearby that was perfect for the occasion—they could easily settle into a rhythm and crank out half a dozen or so ten-minute loops until it was time to call it a day.

When Scott got back to the lodge, his wife, Stacey, asked, "Wasn't that amazing!?" It turned out that Stacey had also gone to the lake for a stroll and had come upon a couple dozen women celebrating the Diwali festival. Clad in bright yellow and red wraps and head scarves, they squatted next to the lakeside trail with big bowls of bananas, melons, other fruits, vegetables, and flowers as offerings.

Scott can relay these details thanks to a photo Stacey took. He hadn't noticed them—not on the first loop around the lake, or the third, or any other one. Without making a conscious decision to do so, he'd been entirely focused on his run.

There are far loftier examples of intense concentration in running history. Both winners of the 2018 Boston Marathon, which was run in an apocalyptic rain-and-wind storm, didn't know they had taken the lead until well after doing so. Deena Kastor didn't realize she was in the bronze-medal position in the 2004 Olympic marathon until the final 100 meters. In chapter 1, we introduced the idea of focusing on process goals, and why this is more helpful during an event than thinking about outcomes, like winning an Olympic medal. We built on this in chapter 2 to show how strong emotions, like anxiety, can lead us to focus on distracting and irrelevant information. In this chapter, we'll look at how successful athletes hone their ability to concentrate on the task at hand to the point of seeming oblivious to much of what's going on around them.

THINKING ABOUT THINKING

The title of this chapter, "What Were You Thinking?," is one of the main questions Noel has asked endurance athletes—from beginners to Olympians—throughout his research career. Their answers provide fascinating insight into what athletes think about during peak performances. Noel has lost count of the number of times he has sat captivated as athletes recounted how they struggled with, and overcame, the challenges they experienced when racing and training.

One of the most common themes that emerges is that running fast is incredibly hard, both physically and mentally. This is true for novices and Olympians alike. But what separates the best from the rest is their ability to extract exceptional performances through a process of deep focus and concentration. These athletes know what they need to focus on and, more importantly, have the mental tools in their kit to do it. Take this example from an elite cross-country runner whom Noel interviewed in 2015 following one of her toughest races:

> I went through 2 and 4 [kilometers] on the back of the leading group. And going into the third lap, I started falling off the leading group. And it was everything for me to stay attached [because I was distracted by a spectator] and suddenly I just lost a second's concentration, and it was like, "Don't lose concentration, concentrate now," and I covered the move. I finished second in that race. But if I had fallen off that group, I wouldn't have gotten back on and that would have been it.[1]

Triumph in a footrace often requires the athlete to win the battle that takes place within her own mind. For athletes like the one quoted above, this means resisting a range of different distractions. Some are external, like a spectator who momentarily captures the athlete's attention. Others are internal thoughts, like worry or the sometimes-irresistible urge to stop or quit.

So how do they do it? What tools do athletes use to remain focused and on task? Just as important, how do they get their concentration back if they lose it?

The first answers to these questions began to emerge in the late 1970s. Across a series of studies, psychologist William Morgan and exercise physiologist Michael Pollock interviewed recreational and elite distance runners to discover what they focused on during training and competition.

Their findings revealed that national- and world-class marathoners adopted what Morgan and Pollock called an *associative strategy.* As described in a classic study, these runners "paid very close attention to bodily input such as feelings and sensations arising in their feet, calves, and thighs, as well as their respiration; . . . [their] pace was largely governed by 'reading their bodies'; . . . [and] they constantly reminded or told themselves to 'relax,' 'stay loose,' and so forth."[2]

The details of what elite runners paid attention to when racing surprised the research team. Up until this point, the consensus was that it was best to tune out from bodily sensations. After all, if running fast was hard, then surely paying less attention to physical feelings would be better than focusing in on them?

But Morgan and Pollock soon realized that these elite marathoners were different from the recreational athletes they usually interviewed. Not only were their physical performances miles apart, literally and figuratively; so, too, were their mental strategies. What non-elites preferred to do was adopt a range of distraction strategies. In other words, they preferred to tune out from the physical sensations they experienced. They did so by thinking about past memories, imagining listening to music, singing, or, for one runner, visualizing stepping on the faces of two coworkers she detested.

With these two separate ways of thinking, we've now got a dilemma! What is the best way for athletes to think? Which type of strategy helps most: tuning out or tuning in? These were the questions that grabbed Noel's attention when he began to plot his PhD research at the University of Limerick in Ireland in late 2012. By 2014, he had published a review of 112 studies on the attentional strategies of endurance athletes—that is, what they focus their attention on.[3] In it, he sifted through the evidence supporting distraction, on the one hand, and association, on the other.

THE CASE FOR TUNING OUT

Before we can answer this question, we first need to consider a much simpler one. What do we mean by "best"? If better—that is, faster—performance is the goal, then athletes probably want to avoid being distracted at all costs.

But that's not the full picture. In Noel's review, he noted that distractions, such as daydreaming, conversing with a training partner, or focusing on scenic views, can help to reduce boredom and make a run more enjoyable. In other words, when the outcomes are less about going faster and more about feeling better, then distraction is best. A recreational runner whom Noel interviewed put it like this:

> My mind just wanders whenever I'm out. It's as if it's a freedom. It's my time and it's me thinking about my things, you know? You're not sitting in the house or you're not working or you're not thinking about things. You're just thinking about *your* things.[4]

What these insights tell us is that distraction has its place in our mental tool kit. It can be a useful way to manage our emotions, especially when we need to switch off, chill out, and get away from it all. One great way to do this is to spend time in natural spaces, such as the countryside or a park.

To explore the power of natural settings to change how we feel, researchers in Scotland had twelve students complete a solo twenty-five-minute walk through the city of Edinburgh.[5] Along the route each walker navigated a congested urban shopping street, then traversed a peaceful, leafy park, before finally negotiating a noisy street in a busy commercial district. Each student wore a mobile electroencephalography (EEG) headset that recorded brain activity to show the different emotional states the student experienced along the walk.

During the park phase of the walk, the students felt calmer and less frustrated. They also experienced higher meditative states when walking in the park than when walking in the shopping street and commercial district. Both of these busier areas demanded greater levels of alertness and attention. These findings show that nature can have a calming and restorative effect, giving our mind a rest from the intense and mentally fatiguing focus and concentration required in much of our day-to-day lives.

A similar study led by a team from Stanford University delved deeper into the effects of nature on our thoughts.[6] For this research, thirty-eight people did a ninety-minute walk either in a parkland setting or through the busiest thoroughfare in Palo Alto, California. The main outcome of interest was participants' level of rumination, a cycle of repetitive negative thoughts about the self that can lead to poorer mental health.

The study included two measures of rumination: a self-reported scale with questions such as, "My attention is often focused on aspects of myself I wish I'd stop thinking about," and a brain scan to measure levels of activity in a region of the brain linked with rumination, the subgenual prefrontal cortex. Both measures were recorded before and immediately after the walks.

Those who did the parkland walk reported lower levels of rumination. The post-walk brain scan results also backed this up, with lower levels of activity found in the subgenual prefrontal cortices of the nature walkers. For the urban Palo Alto walkers, however, no such changes were found. Their levels of rumination were just as high as they had been before their walk. What this study adds is that natural settings can help us get away from our daily hassles and break a cycle of ruminative thoughts. Our takeaway from these two studies: Sometimes, the path to feeling better can be a walk in the park!

Thanks to research led by Tadhg MacIntyre, PhD, we're learning that athletes use natural spaces in a similar way.[7] For some, nature's restorative powers help them prepare mentally for competition. As three-time Olympic ski jumper Andreas Küttel puts it, "Nature . . . gives me absolutely a lot of energy on a daily basis but also for special occasions it gives you calmness." The ability of natural spaces to help us de-stress is reinforced by former Irish rugby union player Rosie Foley, who enthuses, "The emotions are just pure relaxation and just that lovely feeling of this is where I'm supposed to be!"

But this is only half the story. Although positive distractions like nature have benefits, performing to the best of their capabilities is a more immediate priority for athletes during competition. In these instances, tuning in might be a better approach than tuning out.

THE CASE FOR TUNING IN

When Noel dug deeper into the results of more than thirty-five years of research, he soon discovered that the effects of association strategies on performance were much more nuanced than previously thought. When athletes focused excessively on bodily sensations like breathing or muscle soreness, their performance suffered. Doing so made tasks feel harder. In contrast, strategies like keeping relaxed or optimizing movement technique improved performance, sometimes without increasing how hard a task felt.

An intricate study involving sixty experienced runners helps to explain some of these nuances.[8] These individuals completed three 5-kilometer runs, once on a laboratory treadmill, once on a 200-meter indoor running track, and once on a flat outdoor road route. Half the runners—the association group—were asked to tune in every thirty seconds during each run to the heart rate and pace readings on their watch. The other half were assigned to a distraction strategy of listening to music through headphones. All participants were instructed to run as fast as they would like during each 5-kilometer run. The research team also recorded how good or bad runners felt, how hard each run was perceived to be, and their final 5-kilometer times.

In line with research on other distraction strategies, the findings revealed that those who listened to music felt calmer and more tranquil during their runs. Runners also felt better when running outdoors than they did in the indoor settings.

In terms of performance, however, runners in the heart rate and pace-monitoring group ran faster than the music group by an average of 1 minute and 47 seconds. In a sport in which participants obsess over every second of a race time, that's a significant difference!

Just as interesting were the effects of location on performance. Although 5-kilometer times were *slower* on the treadmill than both the track (by 3 minutes and 46 seconds) and the road route (by 4 minutes and 2 seconds), running on the treadmill felt *hardest*! This was most likely because of the treadmill environment, devoid of mental stimulation or distraction. In this setting, athletes probably focused on little else other than how tough their run felt. In contrast, running the outdoor road route, the fastest location of all, felt easiest.

The authors concluded that periodically monitoring bodily sensations and tuning in to a pace consistent with one's abilities allows for better performance. In contrast, tuning out might result in a slower pace but can help make an activity feel more pleasant. In effect, our focus matters, and when best performance is a priority, then having the mental skill to focus effectively is essential.

We can all benefit from the findings of these studies with athletes—and from learning how to focus like a successful one. Lapses in attention not only harm sporting performance—as the cross-country runner Noel interviewed in 2015 attested to—but are also a major risk factor in other areas like traffic accidents. The danger of distractions, such as cell phone use, is well established; one survey suggested that avoiding cell phone use could have reduced the number of car crashes in the United States in 2008 by 22 percent, or 1.3 million.[9]

But phones aren't the only dangerous distraction for drivers. Just as we learned from the beginner runner whom Noel interviewed, a wandering mind can be a distracter too. Although this can be pleasant when we are exercising, the devastating effects of being distracted by our own thoughts when driving were revealed in interviews with 955 patients admitted to the University Hospital in Bordeaux, France, between April 2010 and August 2011.[10] After assessing whether each patient was responsible for the crash that hospitalized him or her (453 were), the researchers asked participants to describe the content and intensity of their thoughts just before their accident occurred.

Drivers who experienced highly distracting thoughts were more than twice as likely to have been responsible for an accident than those who reported no distracting thoughts. Other risk factors contributed to these accidents, including cell phone use, alcohol use, and sleep deprivation. But the finding that drivers' own thoughts added to the risk was new.

Learning to think like an athlete can help here, too. Among the interventions the researchers suggested to reduce the potentially lethal effects of distracting thoughts were strategies to train drivers' concentration skills—in effect, tools to help them retain focus, or regain it when it is momentarily lost. One technique was mindfulness, a tool many athletes have refined through years of practice and experience.

TUNING IN TO THE PRESENT MOMENT

Mindfulness is a trainable attention-focusing technique. When we're being mindful, we are noticing our own thoughts and feelings, or external distractions, but aren't judging or reacting to them in any way. Although we remain aware of these experiences, by being mindful we also detach from them and stay focused on task-relevant information in the present moment.

A great example of an athlete staying on task, and avoiding distraction, comes from the 2019 US Open tennis final. In this match, nineteen-year-old Canadian Bianca

Andreescu appeared in her first Grand Slam final against the pre-tournament favorite, Serena Williams. The contest was played out in front of a vociferous crowd of twenty-three thousand willing Williams on to equal Margaret Court's all-time record of twenty-four Grand Slam titles. Despite the occasion, and a determined opponent, Andreescu retained a disciplined focus to win the match in straight sets, 6–3, 7–5. In her post-match interview, Andreescu recounted how she handled the experience to capture her first Grand Slam title:

> I was just in awe of how loud the US Open crowd can get. It was crazy but I was glad to witness it because that's what makes this tournament so special. At that point, you can only focus on what you can control, and that was my attitude towards it. I kept my composure, which is why I think I dealt with that whole scenario really well.[11]

So how can you learn to think in this way? How can you learn to remain focused and avoid the perils of distraction? Well, actually, you got a head start in the previous chapter. The 5-4-3-2-1 grounding technique that Scott practiced during his four-hour run is one mindfulness strategy you can use to refocus your attention. Many mindfulness interventions have been developed to improve athletes' concentration skills. A brief overview of one of these programs, the Mindfulness-Acceptance-Commitment (MAC) approach, will provide insight into some of the activities involved.[12]

The first phase of the MAC program is educational in nature and sets out to explain what mindfulness is. Activities include a discussion of best and worst performances to help individuals recognize how their responses to thoughts, feelings, or external events can affect their performance.

To follow along, you might find it useful at this point to reflect on some of your own best and worst moments, whatever the setting was. When you performed at your best, what were you focusing on, what were your thoughts and feelings, and how did you react to them? Were your reactions helpful or unhelpful in that moment?

Once you've done this, complete the same process for your worst performances. What you might realize is that you focused on different information, or reacted differently to your thoughts and feelings, during poorer performances. In fact, just as we suggested in chapter 2, you might reflect that it's often not the situation that's good or bad; instead, it's your thoughts and how you react to events that matter. This insight is important. Through this process of reflection you can identify task-relevant cues you should focus on, and which distracting thoughts and reactions might interfere with your performance. It's these task-relevant cues that Bianca Andreescu had in mind when she said, "You can only focus on what you can control." But don't worry if you're not sure which these cues might be. We'll give you a tool to identify them later in this chapter.

The second phase of the MAC program involves practicing self-observation skills. In particular, this phase helps us to become more aware of when we get distracted by irrelevant thoughts.

In this phase of the program, a concept is introduced to help us distinguish between ourselves and our thoughts: the metaphor of "the sky and the weather."[13] In this metaphor, our observing self is the sky, and our thoughts and feelings are the weather. The weather, like our thoughts and feelings, can be pleasant. But it can also be turbulent. Regardless, these weather events, like thoughts and feelings, come and go. Whatever the weather is like at any moment, the sky—our observing self—remains unchanged, sometimes hidden but always there.

In other words, we are not our thoughts and feelings. This is the essence of mindful awareness and focus. By practicing self-observation skills, we can become more aware of our thoughts and feelings in various day-to-day situations, while being able to tune in and attend only to those that are relevant in any given moment.

Once we've developed mindful awareness and attention skills, phase three emphasizes practicing nonjudgmental and nonreactive acceptance. A key purpose of this phase is to help us disconnect our thoughts from subsequent feelings.

Here's an example: Before a competition, exam, or job interview, you might experience a thought like, "I will probably mess up." This thought might lead to feelings of anxiety or panic. In the previous chapter, we introduced reappraisal as a tool to help change an unhelpful thought like this. You might reappraise the situation and think, "I've prepared well and I'm ready for this." This reappraisal can help to lower feelings of anxiety. But this isn't always easy to do. In some situations you will find it difficult to challenge or change unhelpful thoughts.

Mindfulness takes a different approach. Instead of attempting to change unhelpful thoughts, mindful acceptance means that we observe and fully experience these thoughts and the feelings they might bring. Accepting thoughts and understanding that they're just like passing clouds in the sky is sometimes easier than struggling against them.

A second metaphor that helps to explain the benefits of mindful acceptance is the "ball in a pool." Attempting to control unhelpful thoughts is like trying to push a ball under the water in a pool. No matter how hard we might try, the ball, like unhelpful thoughts, keeps popping back to the surface every time we let go. Even worse, keeping the ball under the water, like attempting to suppress unwanted thoughts, is exhausting. Acceptance means that we abandon our futile efforts, allowing the ball to float on the surface. It might stay near us, and that can be uncomfortable. But like storm clouds in the sky, the ball—and our unwanted thoughts and unpleasant feelings—may also, eventually, drift away.

"I will probably mess up" is just a thought. "I will probably win the lottery tonight" is just a thought, too. Although very different, both have the potential to distract us or change our emotions if we focus and dwell on them as if they were true. The key to mindfulness is being aware and accepting that these are simply thoughts, nothing more. As you read on and refocus your attention, both will probably float away before you reach the end of this page.

Once we've developed mindful awareness, focused attention, and acceptance skills, the final phase involves integrating these skills into training, competition, and everyday life. As Bianca Andreescu revealed in an interview six months *before* her US Open triumph, it can take many years to perfect these skills, but in time they can become an effective addition to our mental tool kit:

My mom introduced me to [mindfulness] when I was really young. I was maybe about twelve. . . . I don't only work on my physical aspect. I also work on the mental, because that's also very, very important. It's definitely showing through my matches where I'm staying in the present moment a lot of the time. I don't like to focus on what just happened or in the future.[14]

Research supports the benefits of mindfulness training in both athletic and non-athletic settings. A study with BMX athletes found that these cyclists were more aware of and better able to identify and describe their feelings and physical sensations following a seven-week mindfulness training program.[15] These changes matched activity in brain regions responsible for interpreting and processing information about bodily sensations. Although this study was limited by having only seven participants, and no control group to compare outcomes against, the findings suggest that mindfulness training can improve athletes' awareness of how they think about and respond to challenging events.

Similar outcomes have been reported for those performing in the most extreme and stress-inducing environments. A 2014 study found positive results following eight weeks of mindfulness training with a group of US marines exposed to stressful training exercises.[16] The program was designed to develop concentration and a greater acceptance and tolerance of physical pain, distressing thoughts, intense emotions, and harsh environmental conditions.

Following the eight-week program, both a mindfulness group and a training-as-usual, no-mindfulness comparison group completed a military combat exercise during which the researchers recorded some key stress indicators, including heart rate, breathing rate, and blood levels of neuropeptide Y, an important marker of the body's response to stress. The marines who had received the mindfulness training recovered more swiftly after stressful combat exercises. Their heart rate and breathing rate returned toward resting values more quickly, and they also had lower levels of neuropeptide Y circulating in their blood than the no-mindfulness group did. Subsequent brain scans indicated that those who had received the mindfulness training were less reactive to stress and better able to process emotional information. Overall, these results suggested that mindfulness training improved the marines' ability to cope effectively with combat scenarios.

One additional benefit of mindfulness training might be an increase in the experience of *flow*, that rare "in-the-zone" state when we feel as if we're performing at the peak of our abilities.[17] A survey of ninety-two Australian athletes revealed that those who scored higher on a mindfulness scale also scored higher on aspects of flow, including being able to concentrate on the task at hand and having a greater sense of control during performance.[18] Similarly, a study of elite athletes at University College Dublin, Ireland, demonstrated a large increase in the athletes' ability to control their attention—again, an element of flow—after six weeks of mindfulness training.[19]

Although these findings seem relatively straightforward, their implications are profound. What they suggest is that being in the zone—often perceived as a mysterious occurrence that somehow just "happens"—is much more controllable than we previously thought.

BEING IN THE ZONE

Think about an experience, at work or at play, when you were so focused and absorbed in what you were doing that you lost all concept of time. You weren't aware of other people or distractions around you. Your actions felt effortless and automatic, and like the conductor of an orchestra, you were in complete control over everything you did.

If you've had one of these moments, congratulations! You've encountered flow. You might reflect on this episode as one of the most enjoyable and rewarding experiences you've ever had. But you also remember it because it was a rare, almost once-in-a-lifetime occurrence that you wish you could return to time and again. Kobe Bryant, eighteen-time NBA All-Star and five-time NBA champion with the LA Lakers, described it like this:

> When you get in that zone, it's just a supreme confidence that you know it's going in. It's not a matter of if or this or that; it's going in! Things just slow down. Everything slows down and you just have supreme confidence. . . . You have to really try to stay in the present and not let anything break that rhythm. When you get in the zone, you just stay there, you become oblivious to everything that is going on. You don't think about your surroundings or what's going on with the crowd or the team. You're just locked in.[20]

His description of being tuned in echoes much of what we've learned in this chapter. The first to study flow was University of Chicago professor Mihaly Csikszentmihalyi. He described flow as an optimal experience, a state of deep, effortless focus and task absorption. Importantly for us, Csikszentmihalyi also suggested three conditions necessary for flow to occur.[21]

The first two conditions—as presented in chapter 1—were the establishment of clear short-term goals and the ability to receive immediate feedback on progress. The third, crucial condition was the ability to achieve a balance between the challenge of a situation and the skills at hand. Flow occurs when we find ourselves in a situation where the challenge is high, but our skill set is equal to the task. This skill set includes the mental resources and techniques that we present throughout this book.

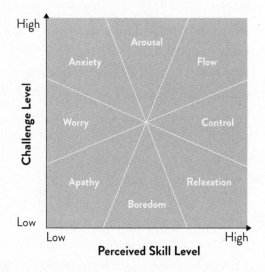

The image above helps to visualize the low-to-high challenge/skill balance.[22] Along the bottom of the image we have skill level, ranging from low to high. Your perceptions of your skill level could be based on the ratings you gave yourself in the strengths profile we introduced at the start of this book.

Challenge ranges from the bottom to the top of the image. Flow is found on the top-right corner, where a high skill level meets a high challenge.

But this balance is fragile. If a challenge is too high for the skills we possess, then we experience worry or anxiety. In the bottom right, where the challenge is low relative to our skill set, we feel relaxed. But this is our comfort zone, and in here we can also get bored. To achieve flow, we need to step outside that zone. This means that we challenge ourselves to ever sterner tests as our skill levels improve or we master the skills required to rise and meet a challenge we're faced with.

WHICH ZONE AM I IN?

Although flow has been studied for more than four decades, we've only recently begun to develop a more nuanced understanding of flow states in athletes. Recent research across a range of sports has suggested that we can, in fact, experience two distinct "in-the-zone" states during our best performance moments. In addition to the traditional flow state, there appears to be a second, more effortful state called *clutch*. These flow and clutch states have been respectively labeled "letting it happen" and "making it happen." What we're beginning to understand by studying successful athletes is that the mental strategies used in each state are different.

The first study to distinguish between these optimal performance states was done with a group of ten professional golfers in 2016.[23] The lead author, Christian Swann, PhD, attended eleven professional golf tournaments and invited any golfer who had played outstandingly to discuss his or her experience.

Those who recounted a "letting-it-happen" performance described a typical flow experience. But clutch performances were different. In contrast to letting it happen, *making it happen* typically occurred when golfers realized they were in a high-pressure situation that required their best performance. To rise to the challenge, the golfers set fixed performance goals, such as to achieve a certain score, and subsequently made a conscious effort to reach that target. Although highly enjoyable and satisfying after the event, clutch situations were also mentally exhausting; players felt as if they had given it everything and used every tool in their kit to maximize their performance. One golfer recounted his thoughts during a clutch performance as follows. How many mental tools can you pick out from his description?

> I'd be like, "OK let's just hit this fairway, one shot at a time, let's stay in the present, you can do this, just take it easy, calm it down, breathe, don't worry about it, it's just a golf shot, go execute it. You can do it."

These accounts of flow and clutch give us valuable clues on how to manage each of these states. Specifically, by knowing the mental strategies that athletes use during their best performances, we can use the tools at our disposal to maintain flow and clutch as best as possible. Although knowledge on how to do this is at the cutting edge of flow research, the hints we're picking up from athlete interviews suggest that it might be better to think less about how to stay in the zone and more about getting into the right zone in the first place.

GETTING IN THE ZONE

Flow and clutch seem to follow different paths.[24] A flow performance occurs after a positive event that lets us know we're in a good place physically and mentally. In turn, that positive feedback builds confidence as everything clicks. During these moments we challenge ourselves to try more difficult things and set open goals—described in chapter 1—to explore just how well we can do.

Intriguingly, positive distractions can help us manage and maintain these flow states. Unlike negative distractions that sidetrack us with irrelevant noise, positive distractions help us tune out analytical or critical thoughts that can interrupt the flow experience. As Kobe Bryant reflected, "You have to really try to stay in the present and not let anything break that rhythm."

On the other hand, clutch performances occur when athletes realize they're in a do-or-die situation, one where the outcome hangs in the balance. During these moments, athletes use a different set of mental tools to perform their best. These tools include setting fixed goals, using relaxation techniques, and talking to themselves in a motivational or instructional manner.

By now, we're getting stronger and clearer evidence that, as we set out in the introduction, athletes' ways of thinking are much more refined than the suck-it-up, no-pain-no-gain clichés of bad sports movies. Instead, successful athletes flexibly use the tools covered so far in this book, including goal setting, if-then planning, reappraisal, relaxation breathing, and mindfulness to help them stay locked in to the present moment. Learning these techniques will also help you to perform at your best, regardless of the situation you find yourself in. But as we'll continue to learn in the final pages of this chapter, we can add still more tools to our ever-expanding kit.

FOCUS ON CONTROL

Earlier in this chapter we promised a tool to help you focus on what you can control. A first step is to think about what you can control and what lies outside of your control in any given situation. Then the important bit is to focus, as Bianca Andreescu did during the critical moments of the 2019 US Open final, on the things you have most control over in any that moment.

Control mapping is one tool to help you differentiate between controllable and uncontrollable performance variables.[25] To complete a control-mapping exercise, simply divide a page into two columns, as in the table below. All the *controllable* aspects of a situation—including things you can influence, if not outright control—can be listed in the first column. All the *uncontrollable* ones can be recorded in the other.

If you were playing in the white-hot atmosphere of a major tennis championships final, as Andreescu was at the 2019 US Open, what might you have control over in any moment? Conversely, what factors would lie outside of your control? We've included some examples in the table below, but you can probably think of many others.

Control-Mapping Exercise

Controllable/ Subject to Influence	Uncontrollable
My mental state	How the crowd acts
My focus and concentration	The importance of the match
How hard I work	The competition venue
My planning (including if-then planning)	The weather conditions

Controllable/ Subject to Influence	Uncontrollable

Uncontrollable aspects include how the crowd acts, the importance of the match, the competition venue, and the weather. Yet we often focus on these things, worry about them, and allow them to distract us from more important considerations. While it's helpful to be aware of these variables, it's essential to appraise them differently or mindfully accept that there's little we can do about them. In other words, why waste our mental energy worrying about them if we can't change them?

Things you can control, or at least influence using the mental tools at your disposal, include your mental state, for example how calm you are, what you focus on, how hard you work, and, as demonstrated by Patrick Mahomes and Michael Phelps in chapter 1, your planning for how you'll respond to challenging circumstances.[26] Before an event, your preparation is also within your control; this includes not only physical preparation but also practicing some of the mental techniques you've learned so far, like reappraisal, relaxation, and mindful attention.

The importance of focusing on these controllable processes shouldn't be underestimated. Research has suggested that a greater perception of control—achieved by focusing on controllable actions—can influence the emotions we subsequently experience. Greater perceptions of control can result in positive states like excitement and flow because we're more likely to view a situation as a challenge that we have the skills to deal with.[27] In contrast, lower perceptions of control—a result of focusing on uncontrollable factors—can lead to unhelpful responses, like anxiety and worry, because we're more likely to view a situation as a threat that's beyond our current capabilities.

MAKE IT ROUTINE

Developing good routines can also help your concentration. Two common types of routine that successful athletes use are pre-performance routines and post-performance routines.

Pre-performance routines include the thoughts and actions an athlete engages in immediately before executing a skill.[28] Having a pre-performance routine can help us avoid distractions and develop a task-relevant, present-moment focus. A good pre-performance routine consists of three phases: readying, imaging, and focusing.[29]

Readying involves directing our thoughts and emotions to create the best state for performance. A golfer might take a deep breath to calm down and release tension ahead of a shot. Imaging involves visualizing an optimal performance. The golfer might visualize the ball going exactly where she wants it to. Finally, to focus, the golfer might concentrate on an external object, like a point on the ball, or on a trigger word or phrase (more on this later) that will help to block out unhelpful thoughts or distractions.

Developing your own pre-performance routine, be it for sport, an exam, work, or other settings, can help to enhance your focus. But a couple of points should be noted. First, routines should be personalized and flexible. Experiment with what works for you, and be prepared to adapt your routine depending on the situation. Sometimes athletes speed up or slow down their routines based on how easy or hard the task is, for example.

Second, routines need to be reviewed and revised regularly. Sticking with the same routine for too long can mean we get familiar with the process and, as a result, get distracted more easily. Routines need to be kept fresh to remain useful.

Post-performance, or post-mistake, routines are also important. For athletes, having a post-event routine helps them shift their attention away from ruminative thoughts and manage their emotions after making a mistake. Tiger Woods, for example, has a rule that anytime he hits a bad shot, he'll forget about it and refocus ten steps down the fairway.[30]

A recent interview study with golfers suggests that good post-shot routines begin with a short period of evaluating the process and outcome of a shot.[31] After this mini review, golfers then divert their attention to distract themselves and manage their emotions, especially after a mistake. They may briefly distract themselves by chatting with their caddie, focusing on their surroundings, or taking a drink of water. Doing so can help them clear their mind and refocus more effectively ahead of the next shot. One golfer described the processes of their post-shot routine like this:

> After [the shot] I would walk into my neutral, reflective box where I would evaluate the process and the outcome, put the club in the bag, and as soon as I walked away from that zone I wouldn't think at all, I would bring my eyes up and just enjoy it.

USE TRIGGER WORDS OR PHRASES

As a final strategy, the things you say to yourself can also help you to concentrate, overcome distractions, and refocus your attention if needed.

This is a strategy many of us use every day, perhaps without realizing it. The "mirror, signal, maneuver" mantra Noel learned from his driving instructor, for example, helps him concentrate on important actions for staying safe.

An example from rugby shows not only how we can learn from athletes—but also how sports teams adopt skills from everyday life. The England rugby union players adapted these cues during their 2003 Rugby World Cup win, when they created the phrase "crossbar, touchlines, crossbar." Repeating this phrase helped players to focus on areas of the pitch where scoring opportunities could be created during critical, pressurized moments in games when they were more likely to be distracted by irrelevant thoughts or events.[32]

Trigger words not only help focus our attention but can also describe how we want to feel in any given moment. One example Noel has used with athletes is "Calm, confident, and in control." Using a similar strategy, five-time NBA champion Steve Kerr, a self-described "overthinker" who dwelled on the repercussions of missing shots, wrote the letters FI on his shoes. That was his cue to himself to let go of negative thoughts and distractions with a "fuck it" mind-set. Think of this as mindful acceptance with attitude! And it certainly seemed to help Kerr. After missing many important shots earlier in his career, he had FI emblazoned on his shoes when he sunk the title-winning basket for the Chicago Bulls during Game 6 of the 1997 NBA Finals.[33]

This example leads us to the next technique that lies at the core of some athletes' best performances. As the Steve Kerr anecdote suggests, changing what you say to yourself can have a powerful impact on how you subsequently feel and perform.

CHAPTER 4

Talking to Yourself

The Self-Talk Tools

———

HALFWAY INTO THE 2012 OLYMPIC MARATHON, Meb Keflezighi was ready to drop out.

The reigning US champion had a growing list of reasons to do so. A longtime foot issue was aggravated by London's cobblestones. Compensating for that foot pain threw off his gait and led to a tight hamstring. He had been handed not his but his teammate Ryan Hall's bottle at an early fluid station. Keflezighi gave the bottle to Hall, who then offered it to Keflezighi. On a humid summer morning, Keflezighi knew he needed fluids, so he broke a cardinal rule of never trying new drinks on race day. Hall's drink didn't sit well with Keflezighi. Hit with stomach cramps, he began fading back in the pack. By halfway, the 2004 silver medalist had fallen to twenty-first place.

"I should drop out," Keflezighi told himself. "My foot hurts, I'm falling farther behind with every mile, I feel like I'm going to get sick. I'm already scheduled to run the New York City Marathon in less than three months. I should save myself for that race."

Then Keflezighi looked down at his uniform, which read USA across his chest. He thought, "So many people want to wear this jersey. They would love to be in your position." Keflezighi also recalled saying after he won the US trials what a strong team was going to the Olympics. "How would it look if you drop out after saying that?" he asked himself. Finally, Keflezighi thought of the family and friends who had traveled to London to watch him race and who were waiting for him at the finish, especially his young daughters. "What kind of example does dropping out set for them?" he asked himself.

After taking stock, Keflezighi told himself, "You're going to get to the finish line no matter what."

And then something amazing happened. Drawing on his years of racing experience, Keflezighi latched on to the nearest pack, because he knew the second half of the marathon would be easier if he had someone to run with. As his nerves and stomach settled, his competitive instincts kicked in. "Beat at least one of these guys," he told himself. Twenty-first place became twentieth, then nineteenth, then sixteenth, as other runners fell off the pace. Success built on success. Soon the pack he'd joined was down to him and a Japanese runner.

With about 3 miles to go, Keflezighi saw his longtime coach, Bob Larsen, who held out five fingers. Keflezighi knew that Larsen meant if he beat the Japanese runner, he'd finish fifth. He tucked in behind his taller companion before dropping him with less than a mile to go. He congratulated himself on fighting back to fifth place. Then Keflezighi looked ahead and saw the green-and-yellow jersey of a Brazilian runner. "That's fourth place," he told himself. "If one of the medalists fails the post-race doping test, fourth place is a medal. Go get him." Keflezighi overtook the Brazilian with 600 meters to go and placed fourth, just over an hour after almost dropping out.

That accomplishment at age thirty-seven gave Keflezighi the confidence that he could still compete with the best in the world. He proved that was the case a year and a half later when he won the 2014 Boston Marathon. In both races, Keflezighi's internal monologue was as integral to his success as the physical training he'd done.

TALKING TO MYSELF

As Keflezighi's experience during the 2012 Olympic marathon suggests, what we say to ourselves can change how we feel and perform in any situation. To think like an athlete doesn't always mean being positive, upbeat, or focused, however. Quite the opposite, in fact. As we've learned in the previous chapters, thinking like an athlete often means experiencing negative thoughts, like "What if I don't perform well?" or "What if I mess up?" As Keflezighi's example also shows, even the most successful athletes experience lapses in concentration, mistakes, or an inner voice that tells them to give up.

But successful athletes have also learned to respond to this inner voice and use a range of mental strategies to cope. For Meb Keflezighi during the 2012 Olympic marathon, it involved taking inspiration from representing his country, reappraising the situation, and reminding himself of what competing at the Olympics meant to him, his family, and his friends. Other athletes adopt similar approaches in the lead-up to competition. Take the following quote from British sprinter Dina Asher-Smith, the 2019 world champion at 200 meters:

Prior to a major competition or race you don't engage with negative thoughts. You don't really think about not doing well or what could go wrong because you don't want to speak or think it into existence. So, you always got to think positively, and you always just have to think about what you're trying to do and what you've trained to do and how well it could go.[1]

Techniques like reappraisal and mindful acceptance can help us navigate these moments of self-doubt. But it also takes time to learn these procedures, and until we do so, coping with challenging moments can be difficult. Here's a beginning runner in one of Noel's research studies highlighting the kind of negative thoughts that are typical for those new to the sport:

I couldn't get my breathing right at the start. My total attention was on breathing. . . . I couldn't do it; it took me weeks to regulate it! . . . And [the things I said to myself were], "Why am I doing this, why am I putting myself through it? I hate this, I hate running! Why am I doing it?"[2]

These negative thoughts—the things we sometimes say to ourselves—are not just reflective of the inner struggle athletes might experience. Most of us also wrestle with these thoughts in our everyday lives. A student taking a difficult math exam might think, "I can't figure this out. I've always hated math. I've always sucked at math. I give up." Or just before a job interview or a public presentation, you may have thought, "I don't know what I'm talking about. Everyone's going to realize I don't know anything. Can I just run away?"

So, let's dive a little deeper into our inner voice than we have so far in this book and explore how we can better cope with the doubts that often surface during difficult moments. To begin with, let's look at what these thoughts are and where they come from.

WHAT EXACTLY IS SELF-TALK?

Psychologists call the communications we have with ourselves *self-talk*. Much of the time, our self-talk is relatively automatic and comprises both spontaneous and goal-directed statements.[3] Spontaneous self-talk can be positive, like "You're doing great!" But, as we've seen in the previous two chapters, these thoughts can also be negative and emotionally charged when we're faced with a difficult or stressful situation. In these moments, the story we tell ourselves, like "I can't do this," often comes to mind without intent. These automatic statements can be unhelpful, causing us to perform poorly or perhaps even quit. So far in this book, we've presented a number of tools to help you deal with unhelpful thoughts. In this chapter, we aim to reinforce the strength of your mental artillery by adding another.

More helpful, goal-directed thoughts are statements we repeat to help us make progress on a task, control our emotions, and, ultimately, perform better. For example, a runner who's struggling up a hill but repeats motivational statements like, "I can do this, I've done this before," is more likely to keep going than the runner whose spontaneous self-talk asks, "Why am I doing this? I hate this, I hate running!" The same can be said for an interviewee whose automatic, negative self-talk leads her to think, "I don't know what I'm talking about. Everyone's going to realize I don't know anything. Can I just run away?"

Using a more positive and encouraging statement such as "I can do this" is much more likely than a negative, spontaneous thought, such as "I can't do this," to help the runner and the interviewee perform better on their respective tasks. So, what can we learn from athletes and the stories they tell themselves to help us through difficult and stressful situations in our own lives?

CHANGING THE STORY: HOW SELF-TALK TRAINING WORKS FOR ATHLETES

With athletes, self-talk is typically either motivational or instructional in nature.

Motivational self-talk (sometimes referred to as *positive self-talk*) serves many functions; we use it to increase the effort we exert ("I'm going to give it everything I have") or build belief and self-confidence ("I can do this"). *Instructional self-talk*, in contrast, involves cues or trigger words. Like the "mirror, signal, maneuver" and "crossbar, touchlines, crossbar" mantras we met in the previous chapter, this type of self-talk can help us maintain concentration or channel our focus.

Our self-talk mostly takes place privately and silently in our own heads. On some occasions, however, we speak to ourselves out loud. These instances provide insight into the type of chatter athletes engage in. Consider a popular YouTube clip of NFL players' self-talk.[4] In it, we hear this monologue from wide receiver Randall Cobb, then with the Green Bay Packers:

> Who do you want to be? Do you want to be good, or do you want to be great? How do you want to be remembered? I just want to be remembered! Courage, pride, determination! Who are you? Let's go!

Later in the clip, we hear Cobb's instructional cues to increase his focus and concentration immediately before a play: "Stay focused, stay locked in. Lock in!"

There's an ever-growing body of research on the performance benefits of training our motivational and instructional self-talk. Take, for example, a study conducted at Bangor University in Wales.[5] Twenty-four recreationally trained individuals completed two attempts to cycle for as long as possible at 80 percent of their peak power, a task called a *time-to-exhaustion trial*. This is a really intense physical effort that most of us might maintain for about ten minutes before having to stop.

During the first time-to-exhaustion trial, all twenty-four study participants completed the task without any specific instructions or encouragement other than to keep going for as long as they could. Before the second time-to-exhaustion trial two weeks later, twelve of the participants were taught how to use motivational self-talk during the task. These participants received a thirty-minute introduction to self-talk immediately after the first trial to identify four personally meaningful motivational statements that would help them at various points of the cycling task. So, for example, during the middle of the task, when they might feel reasonably OK, these individuals learned to repeat phrases like "You're doing well!" or "Feeling good!"

When cycling inevitably got harder later in the trial, however, they were urged to use more encouraging statements, such as "Push through this." In the two weeks before the next time-to-exhaustion ride, these twelve individuals personalized, practiced, and refined their statements during their normal training. The other twelve just continued their normal workouts.

The results of the second time-to-exhaustion trial revealed that the self-talk group improved their time to exhaustion by an impressive 18 percent on average, lasting almost two minutes longer in the second trial than they had in the first. Meanwhile, those in the no-self-talk group performed slightly—though not significantly—worse in their second trial, lasting, on average, twelve seconds less than they had the first time around.

These findings suggest that what we say to ourselves during challenging moments can make a big difference in how we perform. But maintaining a motivational inner voice during difficult periods is rarely easy. Instead, we often experience something of a psychological crisis. In these moments of doubt, we might think about the costs of keeping going (such as all the sacrifices we are making) or the benefits of stopping and giving up (such as more pleasant things we could do with our time).

As the experience of Meb Keflezighi in the 2012 Olympic marathon shows, these crises can strike athletes too. A two-part study on marathon runners suggested that many runners experience a peak psychological crisis about 20 miles into the 26.2-mile event.[6] Perhaps not surprisingly, the first part of this study found that the more intensely runners experienced negative thoughts at mile 20, the slower their finishing time was.

In the second part of the study, a separate group of fifty-five runners received self-talk training to use motivational statements such as, "Stay on. Don't give up," "Stay calm and you will do it," and "I will be proud of myself if I can do it," when experiencing a crisis moment. After this intervention, a marathon performance of these individuals was compared with a group of fifty runners who hadn't received the training. The results indicated that the self-talk runners who experienced a large psychological crisis but countered their negative thoughts with motivational and instructional statements had better finish times than runners who experienced a similarly large psychological crisis but didn't have any effective self-talk strategies to cope.

The important point here is that the runners who received self-talk training still had negative thoughts. In fact, both groups experienced similar thoughts about the costs of persevering, and the benefits of stopping and giving up. But having an arsenal of motivational statements to use in those challenging moments provided a buffering effect that helped to improve the performance of the self-talk-trained runners compared to their non-self-talk-trained counterparts.

These findings agree with the bulk of research on athletes' self-talk. Reviews that compile the best available evidence have shown that motivational and instructional forms of self-talk help to improve performance on sporting tasks.[7]

Interestingly, even though it's often unhelpful, negative self-talk doesn't always harm performance.[8] This may be because we sometimes interpret our negative self-talk as motivational. Telling ourselves, "That's not good enough," for example, might motivate us to try harder next time. In this view, what's most important is the meaning we take from our self-talk. If it's motivational, then it can be beneficial for our performance.[9] Negative self-talk that we interpret as discouraging or deflating, however, is unlikely to help us feel, or perform, better.

The ability to change self-talk that isn't helpful can be critical. The importance of being able to shift from negative to more positive or motivational self-talk was demonstrated in a study by researchers at the University of New Brunswick in Canada.[10] A total of ninety-three participants were matched based on their predicted VO_2 max (an estimate of aerobic fitness) and then randomly placed into one of four self-talk groups: a negative self-talk group, a motivational self-talk group, a challenge self-talk group, and a neutral self-talk group. All participants then completed a twenty-minute cycling time trial during which they were asked to cycle as far as they could.

During the half hour before the time trial, participants in each group were helped to create individualized self-talk statements that they repeated during their hard ride. Participants in the negative self-talk group repeated the type of statements that we might often say to ourselves during difficult tasks, such as "My legs are tired," whereas participants in the motivational self-talk group used statements like "Keep it up."

What was novel in this study was the process used by the challenge self-talk group. These individuals were guided to acknowledge their negative inner voice, but were also taught to follow it with a second statement that embraced their negative self-talk as a challenge, such as "My legs are tired, but I can push through it." Finally, the neutral self-talk individuals served as a comparison group, and repeated statements that didn't contain any negative, motivational, or challenge qualities, such as "The bike is red."

The riders' performance was analyzed for each five-minute block of the twenty-minute time trial. During the final five-minute block, when fatigue was highest—a point where athletes typically try to increase their pace and kick for home—the challenge self-talk group performed best. This group cycled significantly farther—about 200 meters more—during the final five minutes than the negative self-talk group, who, perhaps unsurprisingly, cycled the shortest distance of all four groups.

The authors concluded that the challenge self-talk intervention may have helped participants to acknowledge their negative inner voice, accept it rather than attempt to suppress it, and subsequently focus on overcoming the challenge it represented. As a result, viewing the situation as a challenge, rather than a threat, may have helped to improve the performance of the challenge group participants relative to the negative self-talk group.

An extraordinary real-world example of the shift from negative to more motivational and challenge-oriented self-talk can be observed in a YouTube clip of German tennis player Tommy Haas during the quarterfinal of the 2007 Australian Open tennis championship.[11] After hitting the ball into the net to lose a service game to his competitor, Nikolay Davydenko, Haas can be heard giving himself a stern talking-to in the break between games. But note how, as his stream of consciousness unfolds, his negative self-talk quickly becomes more instructional and motivational. Translated from the original German, his monologue goes like this:

> You can't win like this, Haasi. That's not how it works, not like that. Simply too weak. Too many mistakes, too many mistakes. It's always the same. I simply haven't got the urge anymore. I can't be bothered anymore. For what am I doing this shit actually? For what? For who? Except for myself! What for? For what reason? I can't

do it. I don't get it. I pay people for nothing, for absolutely nothing. . . . [Takes a drink.] So that I can get upset about it? You're a complete idiot! Again, you didn't
approach the net. But you're winning! You're winning
this match. Come on! You can't lose. Fight, fight, fight!

The clip continues to show Haas winning the first point
on Davydenko's next service game. In fact, Haas went on to
win the match by 3 sets to 2, to advance to the semifinals of
the tournament.

As interesting as the content of Haas's monologue is the
way he subtly switches from addressing himself by name
("You can't win like this, Haasi"), to speaking to himself in
the first person ("I can't be bothered anymore. . . . I can't do
it"), to finally addressing himself in the second person once
more ("Again, you didn't approach the net. . . . Come on!
You can't lose"). In essence, when using more instructional,
motivational, and perhaps constructive self-statements
before resuming the match, he seems to change from speaking about himself ("I") to adopting the perspective of a
coach speaking to an athlete ("you").

This leads to an interesting question. So far in this chapter we've seen that *what* we say to ourselves helps us cope
with challenging and stressful events. But could subtle
changes in terms of *how* we construct that inner monologue
also be important?

WHO ARE YOU TALKING TO?

To gain insight into the effects of how we speak to ourselves, some of the Bangor University researchers who conducted the cycling time-to-exhaustion trials mentioned
earlier did a follow-up study in which they had sixteen

individuals do three 10-kilometer cycling time trials in separate sessions.[12] The first time trial set a baseline level of
performance and familiarized the participants with the
study's procedures. Immediately after this first trial, the
participants completed a self-talk introduction and work-
book. During this session, participants identified their
spontaneous self-talk during the first time trial and developed an alternative list of motivational self-statements they
could use during the next two time trials. The participants
recorded two versions of each of these statements: one
beginning with the first-person pronoun *I* and the other
beginning with the second-person pronoun *you*. So, for
example, if a participant said "This is hurting" during the
first time trial, the statement was transformed to a more
motivational first- and second-person statement, such as "*I*
can tolerate this" and "*You* can tolerate this." The personalized lists included a range of motivational statements in
addition to "I/You can tolerate this," including, "I/You can
keep going," and "I am/You are going to finish strong."

During the remaining two time trials, completed in a
random order, the participants used the first-person statements on one occasion and the second-person statements
on the other. The results revealed that, although participants found the "I" and "you" statements equally motivating, they performed 2.2 percent (or 23 seconds) faster in the
second-person ("you") time trial than in the first-person
("I") time trial. Importantly, however, they didn't perceive
the second-person time trial to feel any harder than the
first-person trial, despite cycling faster.

What this study suggests is that both *what* we say to ourselves and *how* we say it can be important. Recall from the

earlier examples how Meb Keflezighi and Tommy Haas initially spoke to themselves in the first person. Then, as their narratives shifted from resignation to resolve, they addressed themselves in the second person.

When we speak to ourselves in the second person, or use our own name, it helps to create a self-distancing effect, a psychological sense of distance between us and the challenging situation we're in. Distancing, and taking a different perspective, is a form of reappraisal whereby we evaluate a situation as if it were happening to someone else rather than ourselves. Adopting this perspective can help to change our emotional response and, in doing so, change how we feel in a situation.[13] The opposite is a self-immersed perspective where we are, in every sense, caught up in the emotion of events as they happen to us ("I can't do it. I don't get it"). Although this is a relatively new area of research interest with athletes, the available evidence from non-athletic domains seems to confirm that it may be easier to change our interpretation of stressful events in the moment, and perform better, by taking a second-person, self-distanced perspective than by retaining a first-person, self-immersed perspective.[14]

Some examples of the benefits of self-distancing come from studies by a team of researchers from the University of Michigan, Ann Arbor; Michigan State University; and the University of California, Berkeley.[15] These researchers investigated the use of first-person pronouns, such as "I" or "my," versus the use of second-person pronouns, like "you," or one's own name to regulate thoughts, feelings, and behaviors before, during, and after socially stressful situations. These situations included making a positive first impression on a potential romantic partner, as one might need to do when going on a date; giving a public speech or interview; and ruminating over past anxiety- or anger-provoking events.

The researchers found that those who used second-person statements or their own name felt less anxious and appraised stressful events, like public speaking, as more of a challenge and less of a threat than those who spoke to themselves in the first person. They also experienced lower anger and less shame, and felt better when reflecting on these events. Individuals employing second-person statements were also subjectively rated as performing better during a public speech or interview. In a nice example provided in the research paper, the authors give insight into the self-talk of one male participant during an apparently anxiety-inducing date. Hands up if you've been there (yep!):

> [Participant's name], you need to slow down. It's a date; everyone gets nervous. Oh jeez, why did you say that? You need to pull it back. Come on man, pull it together. You can do this.

These studies suggest that a subtle shift in how we speak to ourselves, in addition to what we say, can have a profound impact on our ability to manage our thoughts, feelings, and behaviors during a diverse range of stressful events. Perhaps this explains why some athletes refer to themselves in the third person; the authors of the self-distancing study highlight the potential benefit of the strategy on the decision-making process of NBA superstar LeBron James. When making the career-changing decision to leave the Cleveland Cavaliers for the Miami Heat in 2010, James reflected, "One thing I didn't want to do was make an emotional decision. I wanted to do what's best for LeBron James and to do what makes LeBron James happy."[16]

HOW TO CHANGE YOUR SELF-TALK

Now that you know the impact of what you say to yourself on how you think, feel, and act, the next step is to understand how you can change your self-talk if you need to.

There are a number of ways to help athletes change their self-talk. As with the reappraisal tool we introduced in chapter 2, changing your self-talk begins by noticing and becoming more aware of your own spontaneous thoughts. One way to do this is to keep a diary of your self-talk over the course of a week. Important questions to answer as you write include:

- What do I say to myself when things get tough?
- Which words or phrases consistently pop up? Are they negative or positive?
- How does my self-talk make me feel?
- Is my self-talk helpful or unhelpful in that moment?

Reflecting on your diary entries will help you notice the impact of your inner chatter. In turn, this will give you the basis for changing thoughts that are less helpful and, in some cases, downright destructive.

For athletes, many sport psychologists advocate the IMPACT approach to changing self-talk.[17] In the excellent book *Endurance Performance in Sport: Psychological Theory and Interventions*, sport psychologists Alister McCormick, PhD, and Antonis Hatzigeorgiadis, PhD, set out the six steps of the IMPACT approach for endurance athletes.[18] We'll recount these steps briefly, and give examples of how you might use this approach to tackle unhelpful self-talk in your everyday life.

Step 1: Identify what you want to achieve.

The first step is to decide what you want to achieve with your self-talk. This might be to perform better in a stressful situation, to get over mistakes you make, to increase effort and persistence, or to improve your ability to focus in the moment. Identifying what you want to achieve helps you decide what you need to say to yourself.

Step 2: Match your self-talk to your needs.

Depending on the context and situation, your self-talk might need to be more encouraging or motivational. Short, simple statements like "You can do this" or "Keep going, you're nearly there," or reminders like "You've done hard things before," can all help to increase effort and persistence and build your belief that you can achieve what you set out to do. Instructional statements like "You need to slow down" or "Stay focused, stay locked in" might also help you stay focused on controllable aspects of the task at hand.

Step 3: Practice self-talk cues consistently.

It's not easy to respond to negative thoughts, to change your self-talk at first. As discussed in chapter 1, unwanted habits, including old ways of thinking, take time to change. However, the more you practice helpful self-talk statements, the more likely it is that you'll remember to use them when you need them most. The key here is to try out your statements, remind yourself to use them, and practice them consistently.

Step 4: Ascertain which cues work best for you.

Being aware of what you say to yourself is important, but so too is an awareness of the effects of your self-talk. Do your statements help you stay focused, persist for longer, or try harder? Are some statements better than others? Keeping a record of these answers in your diary will help. The priority in step 4 is to keep those statements that work and ditch those that are less effective for you.

It's also important to know that this can change over time. What was motivational in the past may be less helpful now because of how your goals or circumstances have changed. Being aware of this, and changing the statements you use, is important to ensure your self-talk remains effective.

Step 5: Create specific self-talk plans.

You can develop plans for your self-talk using the if-then planning tool we introduced in chapter 1. Using the same formula, think about situations in which your self-talk typically becomes more negative, and plan some motivational or instructional statements that you can use in those moments. Take the following examples for the situations we introduced earlier in this chapter:

- *If* I have a presentation to give, and I am worried that I'll make a mistake, *then* I'll tell myself, "I've prepared well and I know what I'm talking about."

- *If* I find myself feeling nervous and talking too fast during an interview or a date, *then* I'll remind myself, "You need to slow down. Everybody gets nervous. You can do this!"

Step 6: Train self-talk plans to perfection.

This final step takes the practice step to its natural conclusion. By repeatedly using more helpful self-talk statements, you will ensure that they become a more automatic, habit-like response during difficult and stressful situations when you might need them most.

THE FINAL WORD ON SELF-TALK

It's important to remember that doubts and negative thoughts may not disappear completely. Nor should we want them to. Concern, for example, although unpleasant, is considered a healthy negative emotion that can serve an important purpose.[19] As we learned in chapter 2, healthy concern can give us the drive and motivation to prepare well, whether we are facing a competition, rehearsing for a presentation, or studying for an exam. When our negative inner voice leads to unhelpful emotional responses, like higher levels of anxiety, however, it can also be detrimental to how we perform.

Knowing how to change our self-talk and the story we tell ourselves adds to the strategies we can use in those moments. Therefore, when negative thoughts become unhelpful, having a go-to list of motivational or instructional statements can have a positive impact on how we think, feel, and act. In that way, negative thoughts become easier to manage. Effective self-talk strategies can give us a greater sense of control over our doubts, worries, and fears. In the next chapter, we'll show how the story we tell ourselves is one of many tools we can use to build a solid and durable level of self-confidence.

CHAPTER 5

I'm Gonna Show You How Great I Am!

The Self-Confidence Tools

———

SITTING IN THE CONFERENCE ROOM of New York's Waldorf Astoria in September 1974, thirty-two-year-old Muhammad Ali set about trying to convince a skeptical audience that he could, for the second time, become the heavyweight champion of the world. In his way stood a fearsome opponent, the twenty-five-year-old current champion, George Foreman, a fighter renowned for his ability to knock opponents out with devastating power.

As an amateur boxer, Ali had won the light heavyweight gold medal in the 1960 Olympics. After turning professional in 1961, Ali—then fighting under his birth name, Cassius Clay—upset the odds to defeat Sonny Liston and win his first heavyweight world title in 1964. Two years later, however, Ali was stripped of his title when he refused to be drafted into the military during the Vietnam War. Unable to fight competitively between March 1967 and October 1970, Ali missed out on what might have been the best years of his professional career. In his first big comeback fight, against Joe Frazier in March 1971, Ali lost for the first time in his professional career. Later, in 1973, Ali sustained a broken jaw during a fight against the nearly unknown Ken Norton. The popular consensus was that Ali's star was on the wane and that retirement from professional boxing was soon to come.

Foreman had also struck Olympic gold as an amateur, winning the heavyweight title in the 1968 Olympics. After turning pro in 1969, he quickly climbed the heavyweight ranks and in 1973 won the world heavyweight title with a second-round knockout of the reigning champion, Frazier. Ahead of his fight with Ali, Foreman's record of 40 wins and 0 losses, with 37 wins by way of knockout, pointed to his prowess. He had successfully defended his title twice, and many considered "Big George" the firm favorite to retain his title against Ali.

Unfazed by the challenge that lay ahead, Ali confidently addressed the assembled press mob at the Waldorf Astoria and launched into one of the most memorable speeches in sporting folklore:

> It is befitting that I leave the game just like I came in, beating a big bad monster who knocks out everybody and no one can whup him. That's when that little Cassius Clay from Louisville, Kentucky, came up and stopped Sonny Liston; the man who annihilated Floyd Patterson twice. *He was gonna kill me!* But he hit harder than George! His reach was longer than George's, he was a better boxer than George, and I'm better now than I was when you saw that twenty-two-year-old undeveloped kid running from Sonny Liston. I'm experienced now, professional; jaw's been broke, been lost, knocked down a couple of times; *I'm bad!* Been chopping trees; I done something new for this fight. I done rassled with an alligator. That's right! I have rassled with an alligator. I done tussled with a whale. I done handcuffed light-

ning, thrown thunder in jail. That's bad! Only last week I murdered a rock, injured a stone, hospitalized a brick. I'm so mean I make medicine sick! Bad! Fast! Fast! *Fast!* Last night I cut the light off in my bedroom, hit the switch, was in the bed before the room was dark. Fast! And you, George Foreman, all you chumps are going to bow when I whup him. All of ya! I know you've got him, I know you've got him picked. But the man's in trouble! *I'm gonna show you how great I am!*

The fight between Ali and Foreman, which Ali dubbed the Rumble in the Jungle, is not only regarded as one of the most iconic fights in boxing history but also ranks among the greatest sporting events of the twentieth century. Against the odds, Ali won, and regained the title of world heavyweight champion, with an eighth-round knockout of Foreman.

What is arguably most fascinating, however, isn't the drama that played out inside the ring. Instead, it's the apparently unshakable self-belief that Ali cultivated in the weeks and months before the fight. His eloquent monologue at the Waldorf Astoria gives us a privileged insight into the sources Ali drew from to nurture and grow this inner confidence. This chapter will focus on those sources and explain how successful athletes go about the deliberate construction of a stable and robust level of confidence.

WHAT IS CONFIDENCE?

Even at the highest levels of sport, confidence is considered the most important psychological characteristic required for success.[1] Athletes often refer to the necessity of high confidence, the impact of success or failure on confidence levels, and, consequently, the fragile nature of confidence itself. Take this quote from tennis player Novak Djokovic, an eighteen-time Grand Slam champion, after he won the 2020 Australian Open and maintained a thirteen-match winning streak:

> I'm aware of the fact that I'm feeling great on the court. Of course, when you win that many matches, it translates to your high level of confidence. But I'm aware that [confidence] could easily be disturbed, as well, and lost.[2]

Self-confidence is our belief that we have the abilities required to achieve a certain outcome. In sport, this might be our belief that we can perform well or win a contest. In other areas of life, self-confidence might mean believing we can successfully pass an exam, get a job that we apply for, or manage a large work project.

Before we get to the relevant strategies for this chapter, let's consider something about confidence that isn't always obvious. We're not going to tell you what it feels like to be high or low in confidence—you probably know both sides of that coin already. Instead, what we'd like you to reflect on is this: Feeling more confident isn't as random as a coin toss. It's not a quality that relies on luck—something we can't control, that just happens, or that inexplicably comes and goes. Building confidence can be a controllable process; you can learn to flip the coin in your favor by nurturing your self-belief with the best sources of confidence available. This is what makes self-confidence more controllable than you might previously have considered.

In this chapter, we'll set out what these sources are. First, though, a note of caution: Building self-confidence isn't always easy. Like learning some of the psychological tools in this book, the process requires consistent practice and persistence. But if you're willing to do this groundwork, you will also reap the rewards that higher self-confidence can bring.

Before we outline the sources of self-confidence, there's one more thing you should know that might come as a surprise. The beliefs that underpin our self-confidence have less to do with what we're actually capable of, and more to do with what we think we can do with the skills we possess.[3] Sometimes we can be crippled by self-doubt, even for tasks that we're more than capable of completing. You might doubt your ability to answer questions in a job interview, for example, despite having the knowledge and information required to do so. Your doubts might even mean you avoid applying for the role to begin with.

But the opposite is also true. If our belief in our abilities is higher, then we are more likely to try harder or persist for longer on a task than an equally skilled person with lower self-belief. In this way, our beliefs create a self-fulfilling prophecy. We try harder because we first believe we can accomplish a task. And we ultimately achieve it because of our increased effort and persistence, not just our abilities. Thus, our beliefs are fundamentally important to how we act, and higher self-confidence—without changes in ability or skill level—has been shown to improve performance in both athletic pursuits and the challenges of day-to-day life.

This doesn't mean we can fake it. We're not talking about make-believe and fairy dust here! Instead, to build self-confidence—the unshakable kind—we need a solid foundation to start building on.

SELF-CONFIDENCE: WHERE DOES IT COME FROM?

We can trace what we know about building self-confidence beliefs back to the 1970s, when Stanford University psychology professor Albert Bandura published a seminal paper on the role of our beliefs in changing our behavior.* In it, he set out novel ideas about the central role of our self-beliefs in psychological treatments.[4] Foremost was the idea that no matter what the therapeutic intervention, it helped to change an individual's behavior by strengthening their beliefs about what they could do. So, for example, if you believe that giving a presentation to a room full of strangers will be too anxiety-provoking to handle, you'll probably avoid that situation at all costs. If, however, you've learned some mental tools to cope better in that situation, such as how to manage your emotions (from chapter 2), or how to speak to yourself in a more constructive way (from chapter 4), *and* you believe these techniques will help you cope with the situation, then you're more likely to take on the presentation to begin with.

Since Bandura's initial work, we have learned that our self-beliefs affect almost every aspect of our lives, from how we think and feel, to how we persist through adversity, to the lifestyle choices we make. The positive impact of self-belief on performance has been studied in a wide range of areas including education, business, politics, medicine, and sport.

*Bandura studied *self-efficacy*, our belief in our capacity to perform the actions required to achieve a specific outcome. A subtle difference between self-confidence and self-efficacy is that self-confidence is a general feeling, whereas self-efficacy relates to specific tasks, like our belief that we can run a mile in under eight minutes, or write about a topic in an exam. In this chapter, we use the terms *self-confidence* and *self-belief* to incorporate self-efficacy.

Regardless of the area, there are five key sources we can use to develop our self-confidence beliefs. This is important, because knowing the sources means we can draw on each one to boost our confidence when needed. Here's a brief look at each source, starting with the most important one.

1. Our previous accomplishments

Our previous accomplishments—what we've achieved in the past—are our strongest source of self-confidence. These are the solid foundations on which we build!

Previous accomplishments include experiences of success, but they also include learning, improving, and mastering the skills required to meet a challenge. So, for example, learning and improving the skills required to drive a car increases your sense of competence and confidence as a driver.

But it's important to realize that these beliefs are attached to specific tasks. Improving some skills might mean you feel more competent as a driver overall. But you might continue to feel less confident about a skill you haven't mastered yet, such as reversing in a tight alleyway. Knowing this is also key to building self-confidence. Each skill you master adds another brick as you build your self-confidence.

This is one reason we suggest you complete the strengths-profiling exercise found in appendix 1. If you have completed it, now is a good time to reflect back on this exercise. In completing the "current rating" exercise again, you might realize that you've improved some qualities and skills by learning the tools covered in previous chapters. If so, great! And if improving self-confidence was one of your targets, then we hope you continue on to learn and apply the tools we present in the rest of this chapter.

Once we realize that we can build confidence by drawing on our previous accomplishments, it's perhaps not surprising that Muhammad Ali rekindled memories of his victory against Sonny Liston to boost his self-belief ahead of the George Foreman fight. Although the circumstances of the two fights were similar (in both, Ali was the underdog against a fearsome opponent), Liston was a better boxer, Ali declared, than his upcoming opponent, Foreman. Not only that, Ali convinced himself—and told his audience—that he was better now than he'd been in the Liston fight. Remember, self-confidence isn't about what we're actually capable of, but what we *think* we can do with the skills we possess.

This source of self-confidence comes with a caveat: How you perceive a past achievement is important. If you accomplish something but feel the task was easy, or that you were helped in some way, then your self-belief may not change very much. If, however, you attribute an accomplishment to your abilities, hard work, and persistence, then your achievement is much more likely to increase your future belief in similar situations.[5]

2. The experiences of others

Learning from the experiences of others can also influence our belief about what we're capable of. We usually do this by observing others' success. But not always. We can see others fail and compare ourselves favorably to them; their failures can contribute to our belief about what we can accomplish. George Foreman was undefeated as he prepared for the 1974 showdown with Muhammad Ali. But Ali learned—and took belief—from the defeats suffered by Foreman's previous opponents.

Although our own accomplishments provide the strongest boost to our self-belief, learning from others is an important source. It can help to change our beliefs if we have no similar accomplishments of our own to draw upon, for example. So the important thing to do when learning from others is this: Recognize what others did well, understand what didn't go so well, and ask yourself how you might use this information if you were in the same situation.

There's an important caveat here, too: If you want to boost your self-confidence, there has to be some comparability between you and your role model. Learning from a family member who graduated from college, for example, will have a stronger influence on your belief that you can do the same. This is because that person comes from the same background as you and maybe had similar opportunities and life experiences. Someone with no similarities that you can relate to is unlikely to have the same effect.

3. Verbal persuasion: Yes, we can!

Verbal persuasion, or simply being told that we can do something, also influences our beliefs. From a coach or teammate, it might be encouragement to remind an athlete, "You can do it." From a politician, it might be a rousing "Yes, we can!" mantra to inspire hope for change.

Although helpful, verbal persuasion is a weaker source of confidence beliefs than our own accomplishments. In addition, how we appraise what someone says is important. If, for example, you don't truly believe you have the abilities to do something, then persuasion from others will have little positive impact on what you believe about yourself.

The source of persuasion is also important. If the individual is someone you consider credible, like a trusted teacher or experienced friend, then you're much more likely to gain belief from the persuasion that person provides. A runner is more likely to believe the late-race shout of "You can catch her!" from a coach or training partner than a random spectator.

But it's not just what others say that matters here. What is most valuable about verbal persuasion is that it also includes what you say to yourself. That is, the self-talk tool covered in chapter 4 can also build self-confidence. Talking to yourself in a positive and constructive way, such as by telling yourself, "You can do it!" can amplify your belief about what you're capable of. Maybe this explains why Muhammad Ali so often repeated phrases that reinforced his achievements and capabilities, phrases like "I'm better now. . . . I'm experienced now. . . . I'm bad! . . . Fast! . . . I'm gonna show you how great I am!" In contexts like Ali's, when others doubt what you're capable of, the story you tell yourself is especially important.

4. Interpretation of our feelings

Perhaps the least obvious source of self-confidence—and one you might not have thought about before—is how you interpret the feelings and sensations in your body. Take, for example, how you might physically feel as you wait to enter a job interview. As we saw in chapter 2, you might feel your heart rate quicken, you might sweat a little, and you might feel butterflies in your stomach. You might feel nervous as a result, and interpret your sensations as confirmation that you're underprepared, further exacerbating your doubts and worries.[6]

The opposite can also be true: You might interpret a beating heart and butterflies in your stomach as feelings of excitement; a reappraisal technique we learned about in chapter 2. In this case, you might be more likely to interpret those sensations as an indication that you're ready and that this job was made for you.

How we interpret our feelings and bodily sensations can change our beliefs in important moments. For athletes, interpreting physical sensations such as feeling fit or, in Muhammad Ali's case, fast as an indication of how capable they are of performing to their best can improve their belief about how well they can perform.

5. Our imagination

Let's take a step back. What if you're doing something for the first time? You have no previous experience, you have no role model, and you don't know how you're going to feel.

This is a common scenario for many events we feel less confident about. Whether we can draw on other sources of self-confidence or not, imagining ourselves performing well, or imagining ourselves mastering difficult challenges, is also a source of self-confidence beliefs.

Using this technique can provide you with imagined performance accomplishments and thereby build your belief, especially in situations where you might have little or no previous success to call on. Although imagining an achievement isn't as strong a source of self-belief as an actual accomplishment, it can still be helpful.[7] As we'll see in the next section, successful athletes regularly use mental imagery to build self-belief as they prepare for challenging events.

Self-modeling is a variation of this tool that incorporates elements of the second source of self-confidence listed above, learning from the experiences of others. Instead of learning from someone else, however, you act as your own role model.

Self-modeling involves watching video playback of, or mentally replaying, your personal highlights. This can also apply in contexts outside of sport; for example, you might role-play a successful job interview and then physically or mentally replay your performance. Self-modeling can build our belief about what we're capable of ahead of the actual event.

A study by researchers based at Loughborough University in the United Kingdom offers an example of the benefits of video self-modeling. In this study, four soccer players underwent a self-modeling intervention over the course of a competitive season.[8] Before receiving the intervention, the players all selected two soccer skills that they wanted to improve. These skills included passing and heading the ball, controlling it with their first touch, and tackling to dispossess another player.

During the study, the players viewed personalized video montages showing four of their best skill performances immediately before playing a competitive game (a type of video self-modeling called *positive self-review*). The video sequence was updated after each game if a better example of the skill was demonstrated. After the players viewed their personalized highlights, researchers measured their self-confidence beliefs before each game, and skill performance during each game, over thirteen weeks of a competitive season.

The findings revealed that some of the players improved their skill performances after receiving the video highlights intervention. Crucially, improvement in their skills was closely matched to increases in pregame self-confidence. In other words, replaying our personal highlights—by viewing video or by using our imagination—can give us a powerful reminder that "I did it before, so I can do it again."

These are our five best sources of self-confidence. But athletes draw upon additional sources, too. Before we look at tools to build self-confidence, we'll briefly consider some of these sources. We want to reinforce one vital message: If you want to build a stable and robust level of self-confidence, then the sources you draw upon need to be carefully considered.

SELF-CONFIDENCE IN SPORT: THE IMPORTANCE OF CONTROL

In addition to the sources we've outlined so far, athletes get confidence from the leadership of their coach, the support of others, such as family and friends, the environment they perform in, and lucky breaks.[9] But the "focus on control" tool we learned about in chapter 3 is important here too.

If you consider some of these other sources of self-confidence, what you might come to realize is that none are under your control. You can't control the support others give, the environment you perform in, or whether you catch a break. And to develop self-confidence, that's important. If you rely too much on uncontrollable sources, then your confidence is outsourced to the whims of others and the vagaries of circumstances you can do little about.

In fact, of the many sources of self-confidence available to athletes, only two are completely controllable. These are efforts to develop and master skills, and physical and mental preparation. Both of these sources align with the previous-accomplishments source described earlier. This is crucial, because if building confidence is important, then having control over the sources we draw upon is a much better basis for developing a stable and enduring level of self-belief.

This doesn't mean that we should never draw on uncontrollable sources, however. If one or more of these sources are available, and if they're likely to give you a boost, then great! But this is different from relying on them. If you're setting out to nurture your self-confidence, then knowing that you can exert control over this process is empowering. So too is knowing that learning the new mental tools described in this book creates a solid, controllable foundation on which your confidence can be built. Practicing and mastering them will build your beliefs higher.

We can only guess at some of the training and preparation undertaken by Muhammad Ali ahead of his Rumble in the Jungle with George Foreman. We can say with some certainty that he didn't actually wrestle with an alligator or tussle with a whale! But what is incontrovertible is that Ali felt he did something new to prepare for the fight, and that physical preparation likely added to his self-belief ahead of the contest. His mental preparation, including repeated positive self-talk and mantras, amplified these convictions.

Research with athletes has highlighted the importance of developing mental techniques to self-confidence in sport. In one study, for example, sports psychologist Kate Hays,

PhD, asked Olympic and world championship medalists from sports including track and field, judo, diving, speed skating, and rugby to reflect on their most self-confident moments in sport, and where they got their belief from in those instances.[10] As might be expected, the athletes highlighted many important sources of self-confidence. However, all the athletes identified previous achievements, and good training and preparation, including mental preparation, as critical. Yet again, these are the solid foundations of our self-confidence, and they can't be faked!

One elite diver described in detail her mental preparation to build self-confidence before competition, highlighting the role of many of the mental tools presented throughout this book. Which can you pick out from her description?

> I do anxiety-control work and visual-imagery work, which helps to make me more confident with my dives. I also use best-performance imagery all the time in the lead-up to a major competition. I go through my pre-dive routine with my psychologist, and I visualize myself doing my dives to the best of my ability and that helps. I've done that right before competing at the world championships, and that worked well as a confidence booster. Goal setting, and just generally structuring things and ignoring things I can't control and concentrating on the things I can control, also makes me more confident and less distracted by other stuff.

But before you begin to believe that every athlete does it right—and somehow you're the only one getting it wrong—don't be fooled. It's worth knowing that even good athletes don't always draw on the best sources to develop their self-confidence. A 2010 study with fifty-four international athletes, for example, found that demonstrating their ability against opponents, a less controllable factor (an athlete might perform well, but lose), was their primary source of confidence in the weeks leading up to competition.[11] This may explain why some athletes, like Novak Djokovic, see self-confidence as a fleeting phenomenon that can "easily be disturbed . . . and lost" despite a run of successive victories.

But what we hope you've learned in this chapter is that this doesn't have to be the case. A much more pragmatic—and controllable—approach that helps to develop a stable and enduring level of self-confidence is attributed to golf legend Jack Nicklaus:

> Confidence is the most important single factor in this game, and no matter how great your natural talent, there is only one way to obtain and sustain it: work.[12]

Clearly, knowing that higher self-confidence is helpful for performance is important. Understanding that building it is something we can control is maybe even more important. Taking this process to its logical conclusion, in the final section of this chapter, we'll present a number of strategies that you can use to develop your self-confidence.

STRATEGIES TO BUILD SELF-CONFIDENCE

Many of the psychological techniques presented earlier in this book will help to build your self-confidence. These include setting challenging goals and striving to accomplish them (chapter 1), appraising your physiological and emotional states more positively (chapter 2), focusing on controllable actions (chapter 3), and talking to yourself in a constructive way (chapter 4). While these are helpful, here we'll focus on other techniques for tapping into the strongest sources of self-confidence.

1. Meticulously record your preparation and milestone achievements.

Previous accomplishments, good preparation, and mastery of the skills of your trade are key to building robust self-confidence. But the process can crumble when you fail to make the connection between the work that you've done and the challenge that lies ahead. For many athletes, keeping a diary is one way of logging progress. Doing so can increase feelings of being well prepared and self-confident when an important event nears. Nothing helps to ease worries and dampen doubts more than evidence of the work you've done to prepare for an event.

Simply keeping a diary isn't enough. It's also important to prominently record the progress and achievements that you make during the weeks, months, and years of preparation. For athletes, this might be highlighting training sessions that went well, flagging a successful experience like using a new mental tool to stay focused, or celebrating a performance milestone, such as setting a personal record. We detailed in chapter 2, for example, the journaling practices of Serena Williams and Mikaela Shiffrin, who record their thoughts and feelings about positive and negative occurrences in their daily lives. Applying a similar approach, a student might recount learning a new study skill for aiding memory, describe a study session where everything just clicked, or celebrate a good grade that resulted from hard work and dedicated research.

No matter how you choose to record snippets of information about your progress and achievements, the important bit is to draw on them regularly to feed your self-confidence. You might note them in a diary, but you might also attach them to your refrigerator door, or store them in a confidence jar beside your bed.[13] Whatever the format, reading about them—and recalling each event—can help you overcome doubt-filled moments. The key point is that you ensure that your self-confidence is secured to controllable preparation and milestone achievements. These nuggets will provide the strongest sources of evidence as you methodically build and develop that confidence.

2. See it to believe it.

Mental imagery can serve many different purposes, each of which can improve self-confidence.[14] As we saw with an elite diver earlier in this chapter, athletes use their imagination to rehearse specific skills and routines. Performing these actions successfully—even in your mind's eye—can have a positive impact on your self-belief.

Equally, when trying to achieve a goal, you might imagine working toward that goal, step by step, and making good progress. You might also imagine the emotions that accompany a stressful situation, and imagine managing these emotions to remain calm.

Finally, you might imagine overcoming challenging situations and coping with difficult moments while staying focused and avoiding distractions. This might seem counterintuitive. After all, we often prefer to avoid thinking about things going wrong in the hope that everything works out fine. But as we learned from Michael Phelps in chapter 1, imagining negative scenarios—the "what-if" moments—and mentally planning how to respond to each in the best possible way can be a powerful tool in our confidence-building kit.

Some other athlete examples can teach us how to use imagery in a variety of contexts. Explaining how she used imagery to maintain a practice routine while her regular training venue at Florida State University was closed during the COVID-19 pandemic, US Olympic diver Katrina Young reflected:

> Now [in my mind] I'm walking into the pool and see-ing the lifeguards, seeing the coaches, seeing the FSU divers and just feeling at home there and going through a practice in my head. Hearing the coaches giving me corrections and thinking about what I'd feel when I'm trying to make those corrections and going through those. When you don't physically have a pool it's really helped.[15]

Illuminating how imagery can help in everyday life, for-mer World Boxing Council heavyweight champion Deon-tay Wilder has described how he uses the imagery techniques learned as an athlete to prepare mentally for events outside the ring:

> I use them depending on what I'm trying to accomplish. I can visualize myself running an everyday life, having a good interview, having a good day. How I want to approach things. Then when they happen, I've seen it before. I've put myself in the right mindset to react.[16]

3. See others to believe it.

Learning from others—the source of self-confidence we introduced earlier in this chapter—doesn't mean you have to watch their every move, sit beside them in an exam, or follow them through a job interview. Simply speaking to a role model who has traveled a path similar to the one you hope to follow can raise your belief about what you're capable of. You might learn, for example, that you already know more than you realized to pass an exam, or that you have the skill set you need for a job opportunity. Remember, self-confidence beliefs are more about what we think we can do with our skills rather than an objective measure of the skills we possess.

By learning from others, you might grasp how they cope with setbacks, or how they overcame the same disadvantages that you might experience. Even learning from their failures can increase your belief that you can overcome similar obstacles in your life.

4. Get a good support crew, including yourself.

Finally, getting a good support crew around you can be helpful to develop self-confidence. For athletes, support might come in the form of positive feedback and encouragement from trusted and respected individuals, such as a coach, teammate, family member, or friend. In chapter 11, we'll see how Noel benefited from his support crew during one of the hardest running races of his life.

But having a support crew doesn't just mean that you rely on others. Although this isn't a controllable source, what you say to yourself is. Self-talk, which you can master by using the techniques we introduced in the previous chapter, is an important—and controllable—source of persuasion. Sometimes, we forget how essential it is to be our own best cheerleader.

THE FINAL WORD ON SELF-CONFIDENCE

What we hope you have learned from this chapter is that self-confidence is something that can be purposefully nurtured and developed. It's not a psychological characteristic we should consider fragile or in a constant state of uncontrollable flux. Instead, by drawing on controllable sources, and using the tools we've presented throughout this book, you can set about building a sturdy level of self-belief.

Doing so isn't always easy. But the most successful athletes have shown us what's possible when we meticulously develop and master our mental skills. In the remaining chapters, we'll show how thinking like an athlete in several real-world scenarios leads to success, in both sport and everyday life.

PART 2

How to Reach Any Goal Like an Elite Athlete

CHAPTER 6

A Journey of a Thousand Miles . . .

How to Set Yourself Up for Success from the Beginning

———

IN THE SPRING OF 2018, Kikkan Randall was on top of the world. She and teammate Jessie Diggins had become the first Americans to win an Olympic cross-country ski title with their win in the team sprint relay. The accomplishment capped a fifteen-plus-year pro career that included five Olympic appearances and seventeen US titles. It also made up for Randall's disappointing performance at the previous Olympics, when she entered as a gold-medal favorite but failed to make the freestyle sprint final.

By Mother's Day, Randall, her husband, and their then two-year-old son had moved from Alaska to Canada. The relocation marked a new phase in their lives, as Randall, age thirty-five, transitioned away from elite skiing and planned to have another child. As she went to bed that night, she noticed a small hard spot on her chest. She saw a doctor the following day. She was told that because she was young and healthy, it was probably nothing, but she should have a mammogram and ultrasound as a precaution.

The imaging was concerning enough that a biopsy was ordered. While heading to a friend's wedding in Sweden, Randall learned the results—aggressive, stage 2 breast cancer. A week later, she developed a malignant lymph node. Just three months after becoming an Olympic champion, Randall now had a new descriptor: cancer patient.

"I was in denial at first," Randall says. "Then I was frustrated. I'm this strong athlete who does all the right things—I eat right, I take care of myself, I have no family history. Then I went to, 'This is so unfair!'"

As Randall processed those emotions, the lifelong athlete in her kicked in. "I decided I was going to tackle having cancer like I tackled my goal of winning the Olympics," she says. "The steps were going to look different, but I was going to use the same approach."

The start of any large undertaking—preparing for a race, working toward a degree, switching careers, starting a family, or, yes, battling an illness—can be overwhelming. What you hope to accomplish might seem abstract and distant. It's easy to think that what you do on any one day can't possibly matter in the long run. In this chapter, we'll look at how successful athletes create a road map for meeting an important goal, and how they keep themselves devoted to the daily work needed to achieve it.

PLAN THE WORK, WORK THE PLAN

Randall isn't a robot. She talks openly about the full range of emotions she felt soon after receiving her diagnosis. What's key here is what she did next.

"I thought, 'OK, this is real,'" she says. "'Sitting and thinking about the "what-ifs" and the statistics and the fear is not going to get me anywhere, so I need to figure out what I can do here. I need a plan.'"

Because her cancer was so aggressive, Randall and her care team decided to start chemotherapy immediately—six rounds of treatment, with three weeks between infusions. That's a fairly typical plan for rapidly spreading cancer. Less typical was how Randall, drawing on her decades of being an athlete, psychologically approached the process.

"What I did was focus on each stage of treatment," she says. "I tried not to think too far ahead other than having the optimistic view that, yes, it's tough right now, but I'm going to get through this, that there was a good chance the treatment would be effective and I could get back to all the things I love to do, and I could have a long, healthy life.

"So I focused on, 'OK, I have to get through chemotherapy—what does that take?' Well, as I go through chemo, I know it's going to be important to stay physically active, so I made that commitment to myself and publicly that I was going to try to stay active for at least ten minutes every day," she says. Randall, who wound up biking to and from each treatment, says, "This could have been a show-stopping, drop-everything kind of thing, but I figured, Why not be a little open-minded and curious and see how it goes?"

Adjusting to cancer is a process, one that can result in a range of emotions and psychological symptoms, including anxiety, fear, and anger.[1] In chapters 2 and 3 we explored strategies that can change the trajectory of our emotional responses. As suggested in chapter 2, strategies that focus on engaging with a problem and working through solutions—such as reappraisal or expressing our feelings—are more effective to manage our emotions than strategies that focus on avoiding or disengaging from the situation, like suppression or substance abuse.

Some mental techniques can readily be identified from Randall's response to her diagnosis. These include her reappraisal of the situation and her ability to cope with it ("think again" tool, chapter 2). Importantly, Randall's reappraisal of her diagnosis was realistic. Rather than simply trying to stay positive, she developed a plan that prioritized controllable actions ("focus on control" tool, chapter 3), including physical activity to help her through each round of chemotherapy. As we learned in chapter 3, when we are confronted with stressful and difficult situations, focusing more on aspects that we can control—or at least influence—can alter our emotional response to the situation.[2]

Alongside her reappraisal of the situation, Randall's inner dialogue (chapter 4) also stands out. Beginning chemotherapy, and the prospect of six rounds of treatment over four or five months, might have seemed overwhelming. But her self-talk that "it's tough right now, but I'm going to get through this" helped to engender a more hopeful outlook. This, coupled with a mindful, present-moment focus ("tuning in to the present moment" tool, chapter 3) centered on getting through one stage of treatment at a time ("chunk it" tool, chapter 1), undoubtedly helped Randall navigate her difficult cancer treatment.

Research evidence supports emotion-regulation strategies like those Randall used. A 2019 study comprising eighty women with a recent diagnosis of breast cancer found that greater attempts to avoid and suppress emotions were associated with higher levels of anxiety, depression, fear of cancer recurrence, insomnia, and fatigue both before and after six weeks of radiotherapy. Emotional suppression also predicted a rise in symptoms of depression and fatigue during the week after radiotherapy had completed, in comparison with before the treatment began.[3]

This doesn't mean that cancer patients and others facing a major disease shouldn't feel distressed. Emotion-regulation strategies aren't about simply trying to think positively or expecting that we should always feel good. Instead—as with the athletes we've met throughout this book—it's about adjusting to emotional experiences by using effective strategies. These strategies—like expressing how we feel and appraising our situation in a realistic way—can result in more adaptive responses that can lead to a reduction in some of the psychological symptoms associated with a cancer diagnosis.

Randall's care team noticed that her think-like-an-athlete approach differed from that of many other cancer patients. "One of my doctors said it was refreshing to have someone ask, 'Can I run on a treadmill while I'm getting my [chemotherapy] transfusion?'" she says. "I think my providers really appreciated having someone who was so actively engaged in the treatment plan and who tried to be positive and optimistic." (As it turned out, Randall didn't run while receiving infusions—her nurses said that if she got red in the face, they wouldn't know if it was from exercise or a reaction to the chemo drugs.)

STEPPING-STONES TO THE SUMMIT

Steve Holman was the top American miler of the 1990s. Today, he's a senior executive at the financial services firm Vanguard, where he manages a fifty-five-person team and oversees more than thirty billion dollars in small-business 401(k) plan assets. The bridge between those two parts of his CV is instructive for anyone with a long-term goal of any sort.

Namely, it shows that you don't have to get from A to Z in one step. Just as it's best to break a longer-term goal into smaller segments ("chunk it" tool, chapter 1), you'll probably benefit from working toward intermediate but major milestones when starting on a multistep undertaking. Getting a PhD starts with getting an undergraduate degree, finishing a marathon starts with establishing a consistent running routine, and, in Holman's case, becoming a senior executive at a prestigious firm starts with figuring out just what you want to do with the rest of your life.

A 1992 Olympian at 1,500 meters who was twice ranked in the top five in the world, Holman suffered a stress fracture a few months before the 2000 Olympic trials, and lacked the fitness to make that year's Olympic team. At age thirty-one, he was increasingly thinking about the next phase of his life. He and his wife agreed he would give professional running one more go and that he would retire after the 2001 season. But then he got another stress fracture in the fall of 2000. "I could not envision mustering the will and desire needed to try to get over another injury and then try to catch up and get in the shape I needed to be competitive by the spring," he says.

Thus began what Holman calls "my wilderness phase." "When I decided to stop running, I had nothing," he says. "I was stumbling from one day to the next with no direction and increasingly pissing my wife off because I'd sleep until 10:00 a.m. and go eat donuts. At one point, I applied for a job at Barnes & Noble, and I got turned down! I was like, 'Damn, I was on the Olympic team and I can't even get a job at Barnes & Noble.'

"Finally I thought, 'I've always been a good student. Let me go back to school—that will ideally create a path for me to eventually do something." Despite having been an English major at Georgetown University who had never taken a business class, Holman applied to and was accepted into the MBA program at the Wharton School, starting in the fall of 2002.

"Never once did I contemplate doing what I'm actually doing now," Holman says. "Working as an executive for a financial services firm never once came up on my radar back then. But I did have enough self-awareness to feel like I had leadership capability. Like in my athletic career, I figured if I'm focused and put my mind to it, I'll figure out a way to be successful. I had that confidence that no matter what I choose to do, I'll apply that same approach I had as an athlete."

Strengths profiling is a great tool to develop awareness of your character strengths and qualities. You may already have completed this exercise after reading the introduction to this book. It's a technique that professor Jennifer Cumming and the My Strengths Training for Life (MST4Life) team at the University of Birmingham adapted to help homeless youths identify areas of their life where they experienced success, and the character strengths they demonstrated in doing so.[4] The purpose was to help develop resilience, self-worth, and well-being in these young people and help them get back into education, training, or employment—as Holman did.

Once you identify some character strengths, you can plan to adapt them to other areas of your life. For athletes like Holman, character strengths developed through sport might include leadership, teamwork, perseverance, and—through use of the tools presented throughout this book—the ability to regulate their thoughts and emotions in challenging situations.[5]

There are other approaches that can be used to help athletes reflect on their attributes and strengths and, in doing so, prepare a career beyond sport. One approach is called the Five-Step Career Planning Strategy (5-SCP).[6] In many ways, the approach is similar to the future-business-career planning described by Holman, and also the future-rugby-career planning completed by a young Richie McCaw, the "Great All Black" we met earlier in this book ("don't just think it, ink it" tool, chapter 1).

Below we'll present a brief overview of each step in the 5-SCP strategy, but we also recommend that you seek professional guidance from a career counselor or sport psychology consultant if you're using this strategy for the first time.

Step 1 is to draw a timeline from your birth to the present time, and on into your future. Do this on a large piece of paper (ideally, larger than legal-size) to allow enough space for the next steps.

Step 2 is to reflect on the most important events in your past. For an athlete, these might include major milestones, significant competitions, or career successes. Mark each one on the timeline. Reflect on these carefully as you choose which milestones to flag—they'll become important again when you hit step 5.

The next steps are best done with the assistance of a professional, but it's fine to follow along now if you feel this process is helpful. Step 3 is to create a list of all the important areas of your life right now. The list might include sport, study, work, family, and friends. Next, rank each of these spheres in terms of personal importance, time spent on each, and how much stress is associated with each. Plotting the priorities within each area using pie charts, rather than as a ranked list, can help you visualize the importance, time spent, and stress levels associated with each aspect of your life.

At this point, it's worth reflecting on the significance, time commitment, and stress level associated with each area of your life. You might rank family as the most important sphere of your life, but also the one you devote the least time to, for example. Completing this with a trained consultant can stimulate a discussion on time devoted to each area, or stress levels that result from your current life arrangements.

In step 4, we return to your timeline. In this step, important events wished for or expected to take place in the future—such as in the next year, three years, ten years—are positioned on your timeline. As in step 3, you can use pie charts to visualize the relative importance of each of these future events and—as Steve Holman did—identify the key stepping-stones that will take you from your present situation to a desired future.

Step 5 contains three sub-steps. Each will remind you of tools you've learned in this book. The first is to reflect on key moments in your life to date, such as successful achievements in sport, or difficult challenges faced, the coping strategies used, and the lessons learned from these events ("previous accomplishments" tool, chapter 5). It's natural for the challenges and successes you identify here to overlap with the important events you marked on your timeline in step 2. The difference here is that you review these events from a different perspective. For example, you might reflect on what you learned from the tough moments in your life, or the mental strategies you used to overcome challenging situations.

Second, goals for future priority areas (identified in step 4) are set. Critically, this sub-step also involves an analysis of your resources and the barriers that might halt your progress. As Holman's testimony suggests, resources might include personal strengths such as leadership skills, mental tools learned as an athlete, or external factors like a supportive family. A barrier might be a lack of specific knowledge of a career area. This analysis helps you create an action plan, like Holman's decision to return to school to study business.

Finally, to meet the gap between the future (step 4) and the present, ask yourself the question, "Can I do anything today to prepare for important future events?" This can help you identify actions to set short-term goals for (see chapter 1 on effective goal setting) and can also help you to adjust your current priorities (step 3) to your future plans. In other words, as Holman came to realize, achieving your wished-for future might mean that you invest more time in your study sphere and, consequently, less time in other life areas, like your donut-eating sphere.

STANDING ON YOUR OWN SHOULDERS

Here's an important thing to keep in mind when the beginning of a task seems overwhelming: You've almost certainly been there before.

In sports, for example, it's not as if the start of a new season or buildup for a big race means you're starting from scratch. Your body bears the results of all the work you've done in previous weeks, months, and years. Psychologically, you've probably also gone through those tough initial steps, perhaps several times, depending on how long you've been in your sport. In non-sport settings, the specifics might vary, but, as illustrated by Kikkan Randall's and Steve Holman's examples, the overall approach should be familiar.

Certainly that was Meb Keflezighi's mindset the day after the 2013 New York City Marathon. Because of a calf injury that appeared out of nowhere late in the race, Keflezighi had run the slowest marathon of his career, fourteen minutes off what he ran when he won the race in 2009. He hadn't been able even to start the Boston Marathon that spring because of injury. At age thirty-eight, with twenty years of elite running already in his legs, and an Olympic medal and New York City title already in his possession, Keflezighi could have been excused for retiring.

Yet the day after that disastrous marathon, he recommitted himself to the goal he had set on the day of the 2013 Boston Marathon bombings: to come to the 2014 edition in peak shape and try to be the first American man to win the race since 1983. As he hobbled about his hotel room that morning, Keflezighi knew what he had to do to meet that goal. He had already raced the Boston course twice, and throughout his career had run marathons with less time between than the five months from New York City to Boston.

Keflezighi knew that his body wasn't holding up to world-class marathon training as well as it had a decade before. But he also knew that all those years of high mileage and hard workouts didn't dissipate once a given race was over. He had been in great shape going into the 2013 New York City race. He told himself all he had to do now was get over his new calf injury and then build on the fitness he'd spent the last two decades building.

THE RESILIENCY PROJECT

One psychological quality that unites Kikkan Randall, Steve Holman, and Meb Keflezighi is resilience. *Psychological resilience* is our ability to withstand the potentially negative impact of adverse events.[7] As we've seen in these athletes' stories, adversity can come in many guises; events can range in magnitude from relatively minor daily stress, to injury, to retirement from sport, to major life incidents. Adversities can also differ in terms of how long we remain exposed to them. These combinations of magnitude and duration have important implications for resilience and whether we need to call upon it.

A core feature of psychological resilience, regardless of the adversity faced, is the capacity to keep going—to maintain our performance (like Keflezighi), functioning (like Holman), and well-being (like Randall)—despite the obstacles or challenges that life throws our way.

Here's the critical bit: Although we might consider ourselves as either psychologically resilient or not, this isn't the best way to think about it. Instead, research has shown that resilience is a capacity that we can all nurture and cultivate. As you'll see in the rest of this chapter, you've already learned many of the mental techniques needed to develop resilience.

We can display resilience in one of two guises.[8] First is *robust resilience*, in which we're able to use psychological techniques to protect ourselves from the potentially negative effects of stress and maintain our performance or well-being. Robust resilience could describe how Kikkan Randall navigated her cancer diagnosis.

While robust resilience is the ideal scenario, it's unrealistic to imagine that we can display it in all circumstances. Even the best athletes experience moments where they succumb to pressure and their performance suffers. On these occasions, having the skills to respond and bounce back quickly, termed *rebound resilience*, is also critical.[9] It's these skills that helped Steve Holman rebound from his "wilderness" phase.

Much of what we know about psychological resilience in sport comes from the work of two UK-based researchers, David Fletcher, PhD, and Mustafa Sarkar, PhD. In a key study, they interviewed twelve Olympic champions from a range of sports, including track and field, rowing, field hockey, and figure skating, to explore the relationship between resilience and peak sport performance and explain the psychological processes underpinning this relationship.[10]

Based on their findings, Fletcher and Sarkar developed a theory of psychological resilience that took into account four main components: the stressors experienced; how these stressors were appraised and the thoughts that athletes had about their experiences; the psychological techniques that facilitated resilience; and the responses of each individual to the stressors experienced.

For the athletes interviewed, stressors came in many forms. They included competitive stressors, such as training demands, loss of form, or, as for Meb Keflezighi, injury; organizational stressors, such as concerns over funding; and personal stressors, such as family concerns. The stressors ranged from relatively minor demands, such as the need to balance training and work, to major incidents, such as the death of a loved one.

What you might be surprised to learn is how these athletes viewed these events. Rather than seeing them as "bad" experiences from which nothing could be gained, these Olympians argued that difficult or traumatic events helped them succeed in their sport. In other words, learning from these events, and adapting positively longer term, prepared them to deal with other stressful events—such as performing in an Olympic final. One way this can happen is through reflection on difficult past experiences. By considering these adverse events, and how you came through them, you can build confidence to handle future adversities (see "previous accomplishments" tool, chapter 5). A sense of, "I've come through difficult situations before and I can do it again."

These athletes also appraised stressful events as challenges and opportunities to develop and grow. As we learned in chapter 2, when we appraise an event in this way, we judge whether it's relevant to our goals and whether we have the wherewithal to deal with it—as Kikkan Randall did with her cancer diagnosis and Meb Keflezighi did with his calf injury.

Not only that; the Olympic champions interviewed by Fletcher and Sarkar displayed resilience by evaluating their own thoughts in relation to an event, rather than evaluating the event itself. This process—thinking about our thinking—allows us to reflect on the thoughts we have in response to an event, and whether these thoughts help or hurt our performance and well-being. Reflecting on our own thoughts can also lead us to select an appropriate mental tool to use in a situation. This probably explains Randall's strategy of "[trying] not to think too far ahead" and Keflezighi's firm belief that the benefits of his years of training would not disappear in the months separating the 2013 New York City and 2014 Boston Marathons.

These challenge appraisals and helpful thoughts were, in turn, influenced by five key psychological factors. These were a positive personality, motivativon, focus, confidence, and perceived social support. In this book, you've already learned some of the key tools for developing these. Because of that, you can think of resilience in this way: If you have the right mental tools at your disposal, like process goal setting, reappraisal, the ability to focus and stay in the present moment, the ability to talk to yourself in a positive and encouraging way, and the skills to build your self-confidence, then displaying resilience in response to an adverse event can be a matter of using the mental tools that best fit the situation.

The genius of athletes, then, is not about "having" resilience or "being" resilient. Instead, resilience is a quality they've developed through experience, by using the mental tools they've learned and refined—like those presented throughout this book—that enables them to display moments of resilience when it's required of them.

NO BUGLES, NO DRUMS

The phrase above is the title of three-time Olympic track champion Peter Snell's biography. It aptly captures the contrast between the inglorious work that's needed to meet most worthwhile goals and the fanfare that might accompany meeting those goals.

"No bugles, no drums" also hints at why many of us struggle to do the daily tasks that, bit by bit, lead to accomplishing a goal. It's often easy, and satisfying, to picture ourselves having met our goal. We might imagine the immense pride we'll feel and congratulations we'll get from friends and family. But there's usually none of that when it's time to get up early to fit in training before going to work, or when we need to put in a few hours of work or study after dinner. Then it's usually just us and our thoughts, many of which might be about seemingly more enjoyable ways to spend our time.

There are a few keys to regularly doing the tasks needed to meet a goal or complete a project. One key is to make a good start. Unfortunately, there are many reasons we might stall at the outset. We might forget to act, have second thoughts, or fail to do the groundwork required to get under way in the first place. Two of the most common issues faced at this stage are missing an opportunity to act and procrastination. Let's look at how to overcome both of those obstacles.

MISSING AN OPPORTUNITY TO ACT

Sometimes we miss out when the window of time to act is brief or the chance doesn't come along very often. We might miss the deadline for a job application or a rare promotion prospect at work. For athletes, winning a competition often means grasping an opportunity when it presents itself; even the best athletes aren't immune to missing out.

Exactly this scenario played out during the men's race at the International Cycling Union's Road World Championships held in September 2019. Going into the race,

Peter Sagan of Slovakia was vying for the fourth world title of his career, a feat never before achieved in the sport. With just more than 30 kilometers to go in the 261.8-kilometer race, five riders broke from the peloton (the main group of riders). Working together, they built a lead of more than one minute over the remaining riders, including Sagan.

With his title on the line, and realizing he may have left it too late, Sagan made a last-gasp attempt to chase the leading riders down with just more than 3 kilometers to go in the race. Ultimately, however, it proved too little, too late. Danish rider Mads Pedersen held on to win his first world road race title; Sagan placed fifth, 43 seconds behind.

After the race, Sagan recounted his thoughts and feelings about the events that had just transpired to the assembled press:

> I felt very good, I think, but I just missed the opportunity to be in the front. I could've been in the front but I thought the race was going to come back for a sprint. . . . I just chose my opportunity and in the end it turned out differently. I waited, and in the finale I tried, because I wanted to compare [myself] with the others. It was good, just, I missed the chance to be in the front.[11]

Even for experienced athletes, missing an opportunity to act can result in failure to achieve important ambitions.

DO IT TODAY, NOT TOMORROW

Like missing an opportunity to act, procrastination is a delay in acting on or completing our plans. As many as 20 percent of us are chronic procrastinators.[12] Although many of us procrastinate on relatively unimportant behaviors, like getting our holiday shopping done, procrastination can also lead to more significant negative consequences. About one third of Americans wait until the last minute to complete their tax returns, often because it's perceived as a daunting task that people fear making a mistake on.[13] Yet the statistics suggest that as many as 85 percent of people will either owe nothing or get a refund.

Procrastination has also been associated with personal financial difficulties.[14] This is probably because when we procrastinate, we tend to focus on the latest, rather than the earliest, possible time we can save money or pay a bill, and so are less likely to take advantage of opportunities to get those things done.

We procrastinate for many reasons. Lower levels of self-control and conscientiousness—a personality trait—are among the strongest predictors of procrastination.[15] We are also more likely to put off tasks that we find boring, effortful, confusing, or daunting, like completing lengthy tax return forms, than more enjoyable activities.

Imagine, for example, that you're a first-year university student. You're conscientious and plan to study hard to achieve the best possible grades. During the first week of your first semester, you receive an essay assignment that you must submit in eight weeks' time. Despite your best intentions, over the next few weeks you find yourself faced with conflicting choices. You can choose to study, or you can go meet friends at a party. What do you do? Do you stay in your room and work on your essay, or do you spend time exploring the more exciting opportunities that are open to you?

Faced with this situation, most of us would probably follow a similar path: socialize now and delay essay writing until later. That's OK when we follow through on each of our intentions. But in other instances, procrastination can mean we fail to get started on our goals at all.

GETTING THE BALANCE RIGHT

We don't mean to suggest that doing the work to meet your goals should overtake your life. Few of us will be competing for an Olympic medal. Most of us need to balance pursuing goals in one area of our life with a host of other responsibilities.

Here, too, Meb Keflezighi is instructive. He popularized the phrase "prehab, not rehab" in reference to doing things like strengthening exercises, running form drills, and stretching. The basic idea is that it's better to spend a little time each day doing things to stay healthy than to spend a lot of time on them once you're injured.

Pertinent to this chapter is how Keflezighi went about implementing his prehab strategy: He incorporated the various exercises into his main workout of the day. He considered them integral to that training session, rather than an if-I-feel-like-it add-on. Years of repetition made it near automatic that he would stretch before running, do form drills immediately after running, and then go right into strengthening exercises. Doing so meant not only that he regularly did these things but also that he was then free most of the rest of the day to focus on his family and business responsibilities.

Repeatedly doing the daily tasks to meet our goals can, as the accounts of Peter Snell and Meb Keflezighi suggest, seem dull. The solutions to overcoming such issues as missing an opportunity to act, procrastination, and simply feeling like we would prefer do something else, lie in the if-then planning and habit-formation strategies we presented in chapter 1. Planning how you'll respond to opportunities and deal with distractions, for example, can help you avoid these pitfalls. Similarly, consistently doing a relatively boring but important prehab activity can be initiated in the form of an if-then plan, such as, "If I am going for a run, then I will stretch beforehand," or "If I return from a run, I will do form drills immediately afterward."

Once plans are formed, repetition is vital to get these behaviors to stick. Forming habits of the behaviors that will help you achieve your goals makes it much easier to get them done. As we learned in chapter 1, one key to habit formation is to link an action with other activities, so that the habit response gets triggered. So, by incorporating his prehab exercises into his main workout each day, Keflezighi ensured that the desired behaviors, like running form drills and strengthening exercises, ultimately got triggered by the running session that preceded them.

BACK TO SQUARE (AND CHAPTER) ONE

Achieving excellence might seem fun from the perspective of an outsider. And, of course, it can be. But we usually see athletes only in their moments of triumph. In other words, as we discussed in chapter 1, we see the end result—the outcome—and miss the processes it took to reach that point. Athletes' finest moments are often the product of many hours, months, and years of adhering to the not-very-exciting but fundamentally important activities that lay the groundwork for success.[16] It's what Daniel Chambliss, PhD, described as "the mundanity of excellence" in his study into the training practices and habits of Olympic swimmers.[17] As his research paper concluded, "What these athletes do was rather interesting, but the people themselves were only fast swimmers, who did the particular things one does to swim fast. It is all very mundane. When my friend said that they weren't very exciting, my best answer could only be, simply put: *That's the point*."

The same is true for our goals and ambitions. While it's important that an outcome goal be motivating and personally meaningful, the path to success is navigated by focusing on the step-by-step processes it takes to reach that goal. Of course, your goal doesn't have to involve an Olympic dream. Few can achieve that, and in any case, sometimes our goals are much more fundamental. As Kikkan Randall highlighted, sometimes it's simply about enjoying a long and healthy life.

CHAPTER 7

What Are You Afraid Of?

*How to Handle Fear of Failure and
Perceived Threats to Success*

———

IN SOME SURVEYS, people rate the fear of speaking in public as worse than the fear of death.

It's easy to see why—for many of us, we might not ever feel as exposed, in such an inescapable format, as when we have to address a crowd. In this vulnerable situation, we experience the hallmark of public speaking anxiety: the psychological threat that our audience might evaluate us negatively.[1]

Adding to the angst is that, presumably, we're speaking in public because somebody thought others should hear what we have to say. We might have to update our colleagues on a project, memorialize a friend at a funeral, present in front of our peers and professors at school, or talk about our area of expertise at a conference. These scenarios can trigger a stress response similar to the performance-related choke that the New Zealand All Blacks suffered in their 2007 Rugby World Cup quarterfinal, which we read about in chapter 2. Our anxiety means our throat goes dry and our breathing shallows—neither helpful for clear public speaking. We might feel helplessness, a loss of control, and our thoughts might become jumbled in anticipation of a negative evaluation by our audience.[2] Whatever the circumstances, it's hard not to think of the old saying, "Better to remain silent and be thought a fool than to speak and remove all doubt."

Fortunately, most of us who don't cherish public speaking don't have to do it regularly. We do, however, often face similar fears when challenging ourselves. Especially in the planning or opening stages, thoughts of all that could go wrong can be incapacitating. That's true for both long-term undertakings, such as starting a new job, and more compressed events, such as running a half marathon. The potential psychological threats to success can become self-fulfilling and otherwise interfere with our ability to perform our best. In this chapter, we'll look at how to keep these fears from knocking us off track.

O HEAVY BURDEN!

Imagine making the US Olympic track and field team and signing a professional contract with Nike just weeks after graduating from college. Wouldn't you be ecstatic? But might you also feel the weight of expectations that come with such accomplishments?

That was the situation Steve Holman found himself in during the early 1990s. In June 1992, Holman finished his collegiate career at Georgetown University by winning the NCAA 1,500-meter title. Later that month, he placed second at the Olympic trials to make the US squad for that summer's games in Barcelona. Holman was soon touted in magazines and elsewhere as "the next great American miler." That accolade put the then-twenty-two-year-old in the heady company of runners like Olympic medalist and former world record holder Jim Ryun and Steve Scott, who ran the most sub-4-minute miles of anyone in history.

"Almost from the moment those articles were written, I personally felt the burden of that," Holman says. "That was not inspiring to me. That's irrational, but that's how I reacted to it. From that point on I always put incredible pressure on myself to live up to that title. When there were big moments where I had a chance to prove I was the next great American miler, I didn't have the right techniques to deal with that pressure and stress to actually perform at my best."

It's not that Holman consistently failed to live up to his potential. He was the fastest American 1,500-meter runner of the 1990s and was twice ranked in the top five in the world. As we'll see in greater detail in chapter 9, Holman struggled primarily in national championships, despite usually being far more accomplished than most of his competitors.

Performing successfully in sport and in life can, to a certain extent, depend on how we view the demands placed upon us. We can respond positively and view the situation as a challenge or negatively and view the situation as a threat.[3]

When we see an upcoming event, whether it's a competition or a public speech, as a challenge—something we can't wait to get our teeth into—we feel more positive emotions, like excitement. In a challenge state, we focus more clearly, and our ability to make good decisions is improved. Ultimately, we perform better. But when we view that event as a threat or, in Holman's words, a "burden," then we feel more anxious. Our ability to focus and think clearly is reduced, and we think about avoiding whatever lies ahead of us. Each of these threat responses leads to poorer performance.

So, what makes the difference between a challenge and a threat reaction? What can we do—or think—to shift from a threat to a challenge state? What we learned in chapter 2 is that it isn't so much the situation itself that's important, but more so our appraisal of that situation.

When we appraise any situation, we weigh up two bits of information. Think of this as a balance. On one side of the scale are what we think the demands of a situation will be. These demands will vary depending on the event. In a 1,500-meter race, we might need to exert intense effort to defeat equally determined competitors. In a job interview, we don't know what questions we might be asked. In a public speech, we might think we need to say all the right things in all the right ways to impress an expectant audience.

On the other side are our resources—our own skills and abilities. More specifically, what skills and abilities we think we possess and what we think we can do with them. During this appraisal process, a runner might weigh whether he thinks he's fast enough, strong enough, or has the mental skill to stay calm and composed in the heat of a competitive race. You might do the same for a public speech and reflect on your ability to communicate with a large audience. When we judge that we don't have the skills and abilities to meet the demands of a situation—that the demands outweigh our ability to meet them—then we experience a threat response.

Crucially, the more important and personally meaningful the event is, the more intensely we'll experience that threat response. As with Holman, our appraisals might lead to an intense threat response because we reflect that we don't, per Holman, "have the right techniques [resources] to deal with that pressure and stress [demands]" to perform at our best.

Three key factors interact to determine our resource appraisals and, consequently, whether we experience a challenge or a threat state. These are the goals we focus on, our perceptions of control, and our self-belief. As you might have noticed, we've already learned the mental tools associated with each in previous chapters of this book. That's good, because using these techniques will help you prepare for more challenges—and fewer threats—in your life. Here we'll learn how you can apply them to help you prepare for your next important event.

The first factor is the type of goal that we set and focus on.[4] When we focus on outcomes, such as beating our opponents or living up to the expectations of others (people we're not even competing against!), one of two things can happen. We either strive to prove that we're better than others, or we seek to avoid that comparison at all costs, worried that we might be shown up as substandard. Thus, a runner hailed as the next great American miler, but who doesn't think he has what it takes to live up to that standard, may approach a race with an avoidance focus and think, "I don't want to be shown up as worse than others." As a consequence, he's likely to experience a threat response that, ultimately, means he doesn't perform as well as he could.

The alternative type of goal—the mastery goal—involves trying to get better relative to our own personal standards. Instead of focusing on how we compare against others, we concentrate on mastering the task at hand and on developing our own skills and abilities to the highest level we can. What helps to generate a challenge state is when we strive to better ourselves—to learn, and master, new skills that will help us improve.

Many tools presented in this book can help you focus on mastery goals and, in doing so, tip the scales in favor of a challenge state. You can focus on process goals rather than outcome goals (chapter 1). These are the step-by-step, controllable actions that will help you rise to meet the demands of an event. This might entail using some emotion-regulation strategies (chapter 2) to remain calm and composed. You can also work on what you say to yourself by using trigger words or phrases (chapter 3) to avoid overthinking and instead concentrate on the critical steps you need to take to perform at your best. This goes hand-in-hand with ensuring that you have a go-to list of helpful self-talk statements (chapter 4) to manage any disruptive thoughts you might have.

The second key factor in determining whether we experience a challenge or threat state is the extent to which we feel we are in control. We've seen that a higher perception of control—a consequence of focusing most on aspects of a situation we have some control over and accepting those we have no control over ("focus on control" tool, chapter 3)—results in helpful emotions like excitement that characterize a challenge state. In contrast, thinking only about things we can't control—the way Holman focused on the articles written by journalists—can lead to anxiety, worry, and a threat response.

The third factor that shapes our response to a high-stakes event is our self-belief. Boosting our confidence that we have the technical, tactical, physical, or mental skills required to meet the demands of a situation can have a powerful impact on whether we experience a challenge or threat response. But this isn't something we can simply fake. As

Jack Nicklaus reminded us in chapter 5, there is only one way to obtain and sustain confidence: work. Developing our mental skills, by learning how to think like an athlete, is an important step in that process.

Holman eventually overcame his national-championship bugaboo. But he was again weighed down by imagining others' expectations when he started working at the financial services firm Vanguard. Holman—who had never had a job other than professional runner—called on the self-confidence tools he had developed as an athlete to navigate his new environment.

"My ability to perform to my capabilities is 100 percent correlated with my belief that I can be successful," he says. "So when I got to Vanguard, early on I was very, very cautious and timid, because I didn't have a lot of confidence in that environment. I feel like I had the tools and capabilities. Clearly, the people who hired me thought I could perform; a lot of times, people believed more in me than I did myself. But until I got over the hurdle of, 'Yes, I can do this,' I wasn't very confident, and I'm sure it affected my performance."

THINKING THROUGH THREATS

Another category of perceived threats has nothing to do with others' (and our!) expectations. Most of us can imagine myriad ways that things can go wrong when we're trying to perform our best—equipment might fail, logistics might introduce complications, we might find ourselves outclassed by competitors, and so on. We can also get caught up in a vaguer trap of general concern about how things will play out; you might think of this sensation as "nerves," but of course it's a mind-body phenomenon.

Even the most accomplished athletes regularly have to deal with thinking about such threats. What the more successful ones have learned to do is to face those threats head-on in a helpful way.

Consider Brianna Stubbs. A native of the southern English coastal town of Poole, Stubbs became the youngest person to row the 21-mile English Channel when she did so at age twelve in 2004. She subsequently concentrated on shorter, Olympic-distance rowing events of 2,000 meters. In 2013, she and Eleanor Piggott won the under-twenty-three world championship in the lightweight double scull. In open competition, she was part of Great Britain's lightweight quad scull squad in the 2015 and 2016 world championships, where she and her teammates won silver and gold medals, respectively.

You might think Stubbs was simply a rowing machine. The reality is that she was regularly beset by thoughts of all that might go wrong.

Even though she loved to compete, "I would still have dread around how I'd want the results to unfold," Stubbs says. "The thing that's scary about racing is that you'll underperform or, in a side-by-side rowing race, that someone will perform better than you. It's hard to corral all those thoughts and feelings—like what if we're rowing really well 500 meters into the race and there's a boat ahead of us?"

But rather than be incapacitated by such thoughts, Stubbs used what she calls *scenario planning*, and what we've described as *if-then planning*, to calm and prepare herself.

"Scenario planning was a really big tool," Stubbs says about her time as part of a world-class rowing squad. "You could articulate how you'd be feeling and address it, but also you could hear how your teammates would be feeling, and then there's this shared understanding that if you actually end up in that situation, you know what the plan is.

"We even did scenario planning for things outside the race—you're in the warm-up and you have an equipment failure, or something happens and it's hard to get from the team hotel down to the course. If you've talked about it a little beforehand, it's really helpful to get the team on the same page."

Stubbs's planning for scenarios like equipment failure or logistical issues is a reminder of the if-then planning done by Michael Phelps and his coach, Bob Bowman, described in chapter 1. You might wonder, however, how this fits with the "focus on control" tool. Why spend time thinking about events that may never happen and, to a certain extent, may lie outside our direct control?

Here's the nub: Although we may not always be able to control events that unfold, we can plan for, and control, our responses to them. Despite the best preparation and checks, equipment sometimes fails—as Michael Phelps's goggles did in the 2008 Olympics 200-meter butterfly final. Responding to these events with composure—by adopting a mindful, process-oriented focus, for example—is much more likely than panic and angst to help us perform effectively in the moment. As Stubbs says, "One thing I learned was thinking about the finish line as a trampoline—if you thought about the finish line, you bounce your thoughts back to what you're doing now. I learned about being better at staying in the now and focusing on the process."

We can apply a similar logic to our anxieties about performing in non-sporting situations, such as public speaking. In anticipation of our oration, we might experience thoughts like, "What if my slideshow won't open or I can't find the notes I prepared?" or "What if people think that I don't know what I'm talking about?" or "What if my audience won't respond to a question I ask?" (See Noel's solution in chapter 1 to that last one!)

But just as athletes have learned to manage their pre-performance nerves, we can use many of the tools in this book to deal with anxiety ahead of important events in our lives. For example, we can use a relaxation technique like deep breathing or progressive muscular relaxation ("breathe and relax" tool, chapter 2) combined with imagery of progressively more demanding public speaking situations, a procedure known as *systematic desensitization*.[5] The imagined situations might progress from reading our speech alone in our bedroom to repeating it in front of an expectant audience to responding effectively when, midway through our speech, the projector malfunctions and our slides disappear from the screen! Systematic desensitization works by helping us stay calm, confident, and in control during pressurized moments or in response to unexpected events.

We've already learned that reappraisal ("think again" tool, chapter 2) helps athletes manage their doubts ahead of a demanding event. For those of us who experience public speaking or other forms of performance-related anxiety, reappraisal can help, too. When completed with a trained therapist, a reappraisal strategy for public speaking anxiety will begin with a discussion of specific fears about public speaking to identify negative statements and irrational beliefs. Subsequently, the therapist will help the individual to challenge these beliefs and introduce more helpful coping statements, such as, "I can deal with this" ("self-talk" tool, chapter 4), to deal with adverse events or unhelpful thoughts that might arise while the person is speaking.

In many ways, the full reappraisal strategy for public speaking anxiety is similar to the process Brianna Stubbs and her rowing squad completed before international competition. By articulating how they were feeling, and planning how they would respond to adverse situations, the rowers helped one another reappraise scenarios as challenges they could overcome rather than threats to be fearful of.

Other reappraisals can also help. As we saw in chapter 2, an athlete—like a public speaker—might reflect that an audience makes no difference to how well he or she can perform. Equally, reappraising feelings of anxiety as excitement can help performance in both sporting and non-sporting tasks like singing or public speaking.

Finally, remember that many performance situations are the end result of something you've been working toward for many weeks, months, or years. (Champion marathoner Meb Keflezighi thought of key races as graduation day.) If you're a student asked to give a presentation, it's likely that you worked diligently before you were able to enroll in the program of your choice. Similarly, if you're tasked with updating colleagues on a project, you might reflect that you have been given a unique opportunity to showcase your talents.

As Stubbs says, "One of the things that stuck with me most was when you're on the start line and all the nerves are peaking, or really any point where nerves are peaking, to think about how this is a choice and a privilege. We used to say, 'There's no place we'd rather be than right here on the start line.' Or in the hotel the night before, it's easy to think about all those things in a negative, stressful kind of way. But if you think about all the people that would like to be there, you can reframe it as positive."

GENIUS IS 99 PERCENT PERSPIRATION

In addition to having two world championship gold medals, Stubbs also has a PhD in physiology. She's one of the world's leading authorities on the esoteric topic of ketone esters, a product that some say has widespread athletic, health, and cognitive benefits.

"I don't mean to be mean, but sometimes athletes can be kind of simple, and they can just switch their brains off," Stubbs says. "But I was a massive overthinker—it wasn't possible for me to just do that and not analyze and think about things. I had to learn workarounds to being a smart athlete.

"We had very good team psychology support," Stubbs says. "It was available to everyone, but not everyone made use of it. I felt like I was a bit of a head case and that investing in my own psychology was only going to be helpful."

When Steve Holman started having his national-championship struggles, well-meaning acquaintances would try to console him by saying, "You're just too smart, you think too much." As we'll see in chapter 9, long after he had already become an Olympian and achieved top-five world rankings, Holman consulted a sport psychologist.

The relevant point here isn't whether it's "good" or "bad" for athletes to be highly intelligent like Stubbs and Holman. It's that high intelligence on its own doesn't win championships. Stubbs and Holman actively sought to improve their mental skills to be the best athletes they could be. They recognized the importance of knowing themselves and working on psychological areas that they felt they needed to improve.

Stubbs and Holman aren't unique among high-level athletes in this regard. Although many people think of "genius" as an innate ability, what we mean by "the genius of athletes" is that these individuals have learned and honed a set of cognitive tools to meet the demands of high-pressure performance situations.

For example, Olympic ski champion Kikkan Randall doesn't, à la Stubbs, refer to herself as "a bit of a head case." Yet she attributes much of her success to tools she learned at the outset of her pro career, and that she worked on for the next fifteen years.

When Randall was named to the US developmental team in 2002, she and her teammates were paired with a sport psychologist grad student. "She took us through a curriculum of essentially the top mental-training skills," Randall says. "That was great to get exposed to all the different types of skills there are. We started each course with rating ourselves on how we thought we were at it, and then rating ourselves at the end as we knew more about it. At the end of the full project, we got to pick the skills we felt were most important for us."

Sound familiar? Randall is talking about the strengths-profiling tool we introduced in, well, this book's introduction, and that you can find in appendix 1.

Even though Randall had been exposed to some of these tools, like positive self-talk, by parents and coaches when she was a teen, she says, "It was helpful to see, 'OK, that thing I do is helpful, and here are ways to tweak it and make it more powerful.'"

Part of genius is knowing what you don't know and where you would benefit from improvement. With those tailored tools, you should be able to face and address the fears and reframe perceived threats so that they don't keep you from performing your best.

CHAPTER 8

Maintaining Your Momentum

How to Stay on Track After Starting Strong

———

IN A 2017 POLL of 1,159 American adults, the five most common New Year's resolutions were to get more exercise, eat healthier foods, save money, focus on self-care (such as spending time to relax and getting more sleep), and read more.[1]

You can probably guess how that turned out. Up to 80 percent of us quit our resolutions within the first two months of getting started.[2] The figures for that stalwart of New Year's resolutions, regularly going to the gym, further highlight this issue. As many as 47 percent of us drop out of exercise classes within two months of taking out a membership, and 96 percent quit within one year.[3]

Even the most seemingly dedicated among us aren't immune to these depressing trends. Getting knocked off track is commonplace. We might sign up for a race and be fired up for the first few weeks, but then start missing more and more days of training. Maybe we aim to eat five servings of vegetables a day, and after a month start convincing ourselves that potato chips count toward that goal. Or we tell ourselves we'll join a weekly yoga class, or a monthly book club, and six months later are back to our yoga- or book club–free lives.

This usually occurs not because we lack that nebulous quality known as willpower, or because we don't "want it" enough, whatever "it" might be. Starting strong but losing our way more often happens because we don't have the right tools at our disposal to work on this near-universal problem.

ROUTINE SUCCESS

It's in the early days and weeks of striving to achieve a goal that we're at the highest risk of getting waylaid, as we lapse back to our old behaviors and routines. Successful athletes have a lot to teach us about changing our behaviors, sticking to our intentions, and achieving our ambitions.

Consider the daily routine of the gymnast Simone Biles, nineteen-time world champion and four-time Olympic champion, when she was a student at UCLA.[4]

7:00 AM:	*Wake up, brush teeth, put on makeup, and do hair*
8:00 AM:	*Breakfast of cereal or egg whites*
9:00 AM:	*Warm up and train with a focus on "basics and skills"*
12:00 PM:	*High-protein lunch of chicken or fish*
1:00 PM:	*Rest*
2:00 PM:	*Snack of a protein shake, banana, and peanut butter*
3:00 PM:	*Gym work to put together the skill sets from the morning practice routines*
6:00 PM:	*Physical therapy at gym or home*
7:00 PM:	*Dinner (favorite healthy dinner is salmon, rice, and carrots)*
8:00 PM:	*Chill with family*
9:00 PM:	*Catch up on homework*
11:00 PM:	*Lights out and sleep*

All the ingredients for a successful athlete are there. More importantly, however, so are the positive, healthy behaviors that many of us aspire to but struggle to maintain. These include some of our most common New Year's resolutions: exercising regularly, eating healthy foods, and focusing on self-care activities like getting sufficient sleep and dedicating time to rest and relax.

The reasons why we often struggle to follow through on our intentions are manifold. One is that changing our behavior often means trying to overcome old habits, like watching TV on the couch or eating junk food, that we frequently lapse back into.

Changing our behaviors can require a high level of self-control. Unfortunately, as we learned in chapter 1, self-control is a limited resource, and when our self-control resources are low, such as when we're tired or have been resisting temptations for a period of time, we often give in to urges that derail our attempts to change behaviors.

Let's take the most common New Year's resolution—to get off the couch and get more exercise—as an example. Current theories on why we either successfully stick to exercise routines—or start well but ultimately give up—posit that there are two key processes involved.[5]

The first has to do with our automatic associations with exercise. When you imagine different types of activity, do you automatically think of them as fun and enjoyable? Something you like to do and that feels good? Or does the thought of exercise send a shiver down your spine; is it something you think of as unpleasant because it's boring, effortful, or painful (in a non-injury sense)?

Of course, your response might not be as simple as one or the other. There might be some types of exercise you like

and others you don't. Both of this book's authors are dedicated runners. It's an activity we get a lot of pleasure and
enjoyment from. When Noel thinks of running, it immediately fills his mind with pleasant associations, like feeling
free, relaxed, and reinvigorated. It's his "me" time. It also
brings memories of some of his best running experiences
and how he felt at the time. Scott gets so much pleasure
from running that he wrote a book called *Running Is
My Therapy.*

When Noel thinks about golf, however, it immediately
conjures unpleasant feelings. This is because his past experiences of golf have been subpar, usually typified by long
stretches of frustration and even anger while he searches for
a ball in tall grass. (When Scott thinks about golf, he mostly
imagines all the wasted green spaces that could be used
for running.)

These feelings are important, and we can broadly sum-
marize the implications as follows: We tend to repeat the
behaviors that feel good and avoid the ones that feel bad.
This is one reason why Scott and Noel run daily, but neither is a regular golfer!

There's also a second process involved, and this is where
self-control becomes important. Something might not
always feel good, but we still do it. Even for Scott and Noel,
not all running sessions are fun. Doing interval sessions,
hill repeats, or hours-long runs can be excruciating. Sometimes the thought of engaging in these sessions—knowing
what it's going to feel like—makes us want to do an easier
workout, or maybe no workout at all.

But we might also reflect on how the session fits with
our goals and values. Reflecting on our goals might mean

thinking of a race we're training for and that we want to do well in. Reflecting on our values might mean considering what's important to us.[6] We might believe that it's important to work hard, to challenge ourselves to master a task, to maintain discipline, and to forgo short-term gratification in the pursuit of a longer-term commitment, for example.[7] And those reflections might provide enough motivation and direction to get us out the door to start our workout.

But this process—completing an activity that we know won't always feel good and won't necessarily bring any immediate rewards—can take self-control. On days when our motivation and willpower are low, we sometimes find reasons to do anything other than complete that session, despite our best plans and intentions.

There are a number of important implications from research in this area. One is that if you're trying to change your exercise behavior and get more physically active, it helps to do activities that feel more pleasant and that you enjoy. If dancing feels good, or if you get your kicks from playing soccer with friends, then choose those activities over ones that you don't enjoy. Listening to an audiobook or music, or exercising in a natural environment, can also provide a positive distraction that makes activities feel easier and more pleasant (see "The Case for Tuning Out," chapter 3). You're much more likely to stick with activities you find pleasant and enjoyable in the longer term. Much advice on which form of exercise is "best" ignores this crucial matter of feeling good—the best type of exercise for your health is that which you'll do most often.

This doesn't mean it's always fun, however, and there are days when it will be a grind. On these occasions, other tools can help. Those who tend to repeat behaviors that align with their values and goals—such as exercising daily and avoiding potato chips to stay healthy, or reading and avoiding social media to study for an exam—use relatively effortless strategies to stick to these behaviors.[8] The trick is to avoid relying on your willpower to overcome distractions or resist temptations.

One such strategy is to recognize and then avoid scenarios where you need to engage in effortful self-control. So, for example, if you often struggle to resist the temptation of potato chips, despite your goal to eat healthily, then don't walk past the junk food aisle when shopping. As a consequence, there won't be bags of potato chips sitting in a cupboard to tempt you.

Similarly, if you want to avoid being distracted by social media because you need to study for an important exam, or simply want to read more, then switch off your phone and leave it in another room. Doing so means you're less likely to be tempted to scroll through your social media feed and, as a result, less likely to need self-control to complete your study session or reading activity.

Of course, the first principle applies here too. If you don't like junk food, and generally prefer the taste of fresh fruit and vegetables, then eating healthily doesn't require much willpower. Similarly, if you don't enjoy engaging with social media, or find it boring, then you won't really need to engage in self-control to resist being distracted by it.

What you might have noticed in the previous paragraphs is that this first strategy—recognizing and avoiding scenarios that require self-control—is based on the if-then planning tool that we introduced in chapter 1. Forming if-then and coping plans can help you stay on track by reducing your need for self-control to overcome distractions or resist temptations. In other words, you can use if-then planning to create a solution that reduces your exposure to distractions or temptations in the first place.

For some behaviors, like establishing an exercise routine, enlisting the support of others can also help you stay on track.[9] A training companion can make the gym or exercise environment feel less intimidating.[10] Conversing with a partner can also provide a welcome distraction that helps to make an exercise session feel good. Making an exercise plan and, with it, a commitment to your training buddy also reduces your reliance on your own motivation and self-control. You're much more likely to attend an exercise session when you've made plans with a partner, even on occasions when your motivation has waned.

A final, but fundamentally important, strategy to help you stay on track and reduce your reliance on self-control is to follow the steps to form new habits ("make it a habit" tool, chapter 1). By definition, a habit is an automatic action that takes little motivation or conscious thought to perform. In other words, performing habit behaviors relies less on willpower because we don't need to plan or make decisions about these behaviors to complete them. So even on days when you feel tired, had a stressful time at work, or are in danger of being exposed to distractions or temptations, you're still more likely to complete behaviors that have become a habit. As we learned in chapter 1, following the steps to break unwanted habits and form new ones can be useful to successfully change and maintain a range of behaviors, including eating healthily and getting regular exercise.

KEEP YOUR EYES ON THE PRIZE

Unfortunately, however, many of us like junk food and prefer watching TV or lazing on the couch over exercising. Equally, we find reasons to spend hours on end with our social media feed—or other tempting distractions—when we should be working. When writing a book, for example, you might tell yourself your head isn't in the right place at the moment, and that scrolling through your Twitter feed or doing a crossword puzzle will provide just the break you need until you sense you're ready to do good work.

If any of these scenarios apply to you, then these are distractions and temptations that can knock you off track toward achieving your longer-term goals. Although ceding momentarily to any one temptation or distraction isn't a big deal, they can easily become insidious. The cumulative effect of regularly telling yourself "just this once" can waylay you more than failing to establish a good habit in the first place; it can be easier to think of temptations and distractions as aberrations, regardless of how often they throw you off course.

One thing that athletes can teach us in this regard is that the "perfect" time to work toward our goals is almost always now. Training most or all days of the week entails doing the best you can in the time available. Waiting for a platonic ideal of physical vigor, mental strength, and climatic cooperation will almost always mean not getting going. When you feel the pull of temptations and distractions in these situations, remind yourself of all the times you headed out to run in the rain or kept your morning gym routine after a horrible night of sleep. And then get going.

These situations are also yet another reminder of how important good goals are. As we detailed in chapter 1, one aspect of a good goal is that it requires you to push yourself to meet it; if it's something you already know you can do, what's the point? Inherent in pushing yourself is occasionally feeling like taking the easy way out, be that blowing off work for time on social media or sleeping in rather than working out.

Also in chapter 1, we met world-renowned biologist and former champion ultramarathoner Bernd Heinrich. We saw that Heinrich believes challenging long-term goals are part of being fully human; he calls them "substitute chases," modern-day versions of the persistence hunting our ancient ancestors used to wear down prey. Heinrich says that evolution favored hunters who could keep hunting even when it seemed futile, and that we still bear that psychological eyes-on-the-prize trait.

For Heinrich, running is to training as strolling in nature is to research. Training and research require consciously adopting patience to reach the other side, whether it's a personal best or a biology breakthrough.

"Running is fun, but training is not, and sitting in a tree all day watching ravens is not fun," he says about one of his areas of research. "You can only do it if you have that vision, that specific goal that you know in order to get you have to put up with drudgery. With research, it's like running: You have to put in every step to pursue that goal and get that prize."

What Heinrich calls "drudgery" is what we'll more charitably call "those times when you're at risk of losing motivation and don't feel like working toward your goal." A runner-scientist who is decades younger than Heinrich has a similar approach to persisting in sport and everyday life.

Lillian Kay Petersen of Los Alamos, New Mexico, was the 2020 winner of the Regeneron Science Talent Search, a prestigious science and math competition for American high school seniors. (It was founded in 1942, two years after Heinrich was born.)

Petersen's winning research project was a model to predict crop yields in every country in Africa three to four months before the harvest using satellite imagery. "The reason I built this model is that developing countries often have slow responses to droughts and food shortages," she says. "Ethiopia had a major drought in 2015–16 and eighteen million were at risk of starvation. Organizations were unprepared for this hunger crisis. So I wanted to find a way to monitor crop health as drought evolved to help organizations respond in real time and prevent future food crises."

Petersen, now a Harvard student, has done at least one research project a year since seventh grade; two of her studies have been published in peer-reviewed journals. She also started running in seventh grade, and says that the thinking skills she learned through running have been key to her prodigious science output.

"I keep my focus on my goal and exactly what I want to accomplish," she says about hard running workouts or races. "I know that if I slack off or take the easier route, then I won't reach that goal I've been trying for so long to get to."

Petersen applies that stay-on-target mindset to research when, inevitably, other activities are temporarily tempting. "Research is never easy," she says. "It requires continuous work for months or years while I'm trying to do a whole bunch of other things at the same time. You have to be willing to work through the 'uphills'—the really difficult part of research—to reach the top and reach the goal, and then be able to ride the downhill where you get all the recognition and where it feels great. But first you have to work really hard.

"In running, you have good and bad days, and uphills and downhills," Petersen says. "In research, sometimes it's fun, but other times it just leaves you banging your head against your computer because you can't find what's going wrong and it's so difficult you want to quit. Like in running, it's always worth it because you know that every day you train, you're building on your strengths and getting closer to your goals. In research, it's worth it because every day you work on your project, you're building your skills, you're becoming more proficient and getting closer to your goal, be it results, a finalized research project, or publishing a paper."

We'll leave Petersen with the final word on how personally meaningful goals and values can help us resist the sway of unrelated temptations and distractions.

"Through running I've learned the distinction between satisfaction and short-term happiness," she says. "I feel it's worth working really hard for satisfaction. As I work harder and achieve more goals, I find a lot of things I might do, like watching TV or going on social media, aren't worth it to me. It's something you do to feel happy in the moment, but it doesn't lead to long-term success or satisfaction."

CHAPTER 9

The Middle Muddle

How to Adapt on the Go and
Not Overthink Things

———

MUCH OF THIS BOOK is about how to deal with those little (or not so little) voices that say, "Back off," "Give up," "Save it for next time," and other unhelpful things during challenging situations. But these are-you-tough-enough moments aren't the only tests of our ability to perform our best.

We can also get waylaid by two seemingly opposite phenomena—not thinking enough and thinking too much, to put it perhaps too simply. By "not thinking enough" we mean being unable to adapt our mental approach as warranted by events. By "thinking too much" we mean getting caught in an endless analysis loop of how events are playing out. Both detract from performance.

These gremlins tend to pop up not when the finish is in sight and clarity on how to proceed is more straightforward. ("Wrap it up!") Rather, not knowing how to adapt, and not being able to get out of our own way, most often bedevil us in the first two thirds of a challenging undertaking. In this chapter, we'll look at how to handle these occurrences so as to keep working toward the best possible outcome.

ADAPTING ON THE GO

Ryan Hall's appearance at the 2007 Gate River Run has to have made it one of the most highly anticipated 15-kilometer races in history. Hall came to the Florida event less than two months removed from the Houston Half Marathon, where he'd set the US half marathon record of 59:43. The time made him the first non-African-born runner to break an hour for the distance.

Even more impressive than Hall's time was how he ran his record. As would be the case later that year when he won the US Olympic marathon trials, Hall in his half marathon seemed impervious to the world around him. He ran solo almost the entire half marathon, clocking off one 4:30 mile after another with ease, his flowing stride exuding competence and confidence. At the finish he looked more energized than exhausted.

So running fans got excited when Hall said he would target the American 15K record at Gate River. Surpassing Todd Williams's mark of 42:22 seemed a more-than-reasonable goal—Hall had averaged 4:33 per mile for 13.1 miles in Houston, and breaking Williams's record would require averaging only 1 second per mile faster for 9.3 miles, or almost 4 miles shorter than a half marathon.

Williams's record didn't fall that day. (In fact, the mark, set in 1995, still stands.) Unlike in Houston, Hall's body wasn't ready to accomplish the ambitious goal his mind had set. He was off record pace almost immediately. Hall's time for the first 5 kilometers was 14:13, an average pace of 4:35 per mile—slower than he had run for 13.1 miles two months earlier.

Over the next 5 kilometers, Hall not only fell farther behind his goal pace, as confirmed by frequent glances at his watch, but he lost the lead. Meb Keflezighi, whom Hall had beaten by more than two and a half minutes in Houston, passed Hall soon after the 5-kilometer mark. By 10 kilometers, Keflezighi was 14 seconds ahead. By the finish, Keflezighi's lead had grown to 20 seconds, with Keflezighi winning in 43:40 and Hall finishing second in 44:00—more than a minute and a half slower than his goal.

As we saw in chapter 4, Keflezighi was a master of motivational self-talk throughout his long career. One factor in this is that he entered races with flexible, tiered goals, and quickly adapted when it was no longer realistic to chase his top goal for the day. Hall, in contrast, often struggled with unpredictability in races. He often seemed to be competing more against the clock than against other runners. Gate River in 2007 was an extreme example of the dangers of doing so, because once the clock no longer provided positive feedback, Hall seemed adrift.

Of course, we can only speculate on Hall's thoughts during that race. But based on the experiences and evidence we've recounted throughout this book, we can propose some mental tools that will help you to adapt on the go, especially when a situation requires your best performance. Focusing on controllable process goals (like running smoothly and staying relaxed), and less on outcome goals (like breaking a record), can help you to feel less anxious and more confident, both of which are likely to facilitate a better performance. Setting short-term sub-goals, and—as Hall himself put it in the title of his memoir—running the mile you're in can also help you stay in the moment and adapt effectively to changing circumstances. This is one way that athletes apply the "chunk it" tool we introduced in chapter 2.

In chapter 3 we also learned that sometimes, best performances happen when we have to grind it out. Comparing Hall's Houston Half Marathon record with his failed Gate River record attempt, you might think back to the two "in-the-zone" states, flow and clutch, we introduced in chapter 3.

Flow often happens when an early, positive event—like running the first mile within record pace—lets us know we're in a good place. From there, things just click and our confidence grows.

But what about those days when we have to "make it happen"? In those circumstances, when things don't quite click, we have to rely on a different mental skill set to grind it out. Staying relaxed (chapter 2), tuning in to the present moment (chapter 3), and talking to ourselves in a constructive and motivational ("You can do this!") way (chapter 4) can all help in this moment.

And as we saw in chapter 1, the best athletes plan and prepare for these challenges so they can adapt in the moment; recall Michael Phelps's calm, controlled response to a goggle failure during the 200-meter butterfly final at the 2008 Olympics. Planning how we'll respond to "what-if" moments can likewise help us through even the most challenging events.

DON'T BE SURPRISED BY SURPRISES

As with the other skills in this book, you can improve your ability to manage the unexpected. Michael Phelps again comes to mind, thanks to his and his coach's penchant for practicing how to navigate specific unlikely situations. Most of us, of course, don't have the time to devote to purposefully creating "what-if" learning experiences. But you can draw on previous experiences of responding to surprises to boost your confidence and resilience in future situations.

Consider two of the hardest workouts of Alvina Begay's long running career. Before joining the prestigious Nike Oregon Project, Begay had trained plenty hard. But the group's coach, Alberto Salazar, who had been administered last rites after completely spending himself at the 1978 Falmouth Road Race, had different ideas about what "hard" meant. (Years after Begay left the group, Salazar received a doping ban; Begay wasn't implicated in Salazar's offenses.)

Pre-Salazar, one of Begay's hardest workouts was six one-mile intervals, on a road loop, all run between 5K and 10K race pace. Under Salazar, that would have been nothing special. Begay still shudders a little when she recalls a Salazar workout of ten one-mile intervals, all run on the track, with each mile interval to be run faster than the previous one.

Begay got through this workout of a lifetime thanks to chunking, process goals, and motivational self-talk. She thought about only the mile interval at hand rather than the overwhelming totality; during each interval, she focused on hitting the en route split times needed to finish in the target time; and she continually told herself she could complete the monster session.

And she did. Or at least she thought she did. As Begay congratulated herself for finishing, Salazar had a surprise for her: She was now to do four 400-meter repeats (each repeat being one lap of the track) as fast as possible. "I wanted to cry," Begay says. Instead, she reset her focus and nailed the cruel add-on.

On another occasion, Begay was told to do a 12-mile run a little faster than her goal marathon pace. In practical terms, this more or less meant running 12 miles at her half marathon (13.1 miles) race pace. As she was closing in on the 12-mile mark, feeling extremely tired but also excited about how well the workout had gone, Salazar told Begay to keep going for another 2 miles—at a faster pace!

Salazar's tactics aren't unique to the on-track strategies of coaches. In the often-torturous world of laboratory-based endurance research, boffins and masochists-in-lab-coats like Noel have often manipulated tasks in a similar way to Begay's unexpected 14-mile training run.

One example is a study conducted by researchers at the University of Cape Town, South Africa.[1] Sixteen well-trained runners did three twenty-minute bouts on a treadmill. On one trial, participants were told they would run for twenty minutes before starting the session. On a second trial, they were given no prior knowledge of the run's length, and were stopped after the twenty minutes had elapsed. On a third trial, participants were told they would run for only ten minutes. But as they neared their expected finish point, like Salazar to Begay, the researchers told the runners that they had to keep going for an additional ten minutes.

Predictably, in the minutes that followed the unexpected extension to the third trial, participants felt worse than they had earlier in the run. Perhaps more interesting was the fact that—despite running at the exact same pace—participants also rated their run as feeling harder once they ran beyond the ten-minute point than they had at the same time in the two other twenty-minute trials. This coincided with a shift in their focus toward thoughts about how their body was feeling. As we saw in chapter 3, tuning in, and focusing excessively on bodily sensations like our breathing or muscle fatigue, can make an activity like running feel harder. Our ability to manage unexpected events like this, then, can depend on the mental techniques we choose to control our attention in that specific moment.

Noel employed a similar approach for a 2019 study with runners in his lab at Ulster University in Northern Ireland.[2] Noel wanted to know if the difficulty of a running trial influenced how people paced it. He also wanted to learn more about the mental strategies runners used to cope with unexpected events. In a setup similar to the University of Cape Town study, Noel had twenty-eight trained runners complete three self-paced running trials. The first was a flat 3-kilometer time trial. In both the second and third time trials, completed in a random order, participants ran up a 7 percent incline over the last 800 meters.

In one of the trials—a known-incline trial—participants were told before they set off that they would have to run up the 7 percent slope for the final part of the trial. In the other session—an unknown-incline trial—they were deceived. Before this 3-kilometer run, they were told that the treadmill would remain flat the whole way. In fact, they were informed about the 7 percent grade only 200 meters before they hit the incline. In practical terms, this meant that the runners learned of the surprise hill less than a minute before encountering it.

As you might expect, participants ran faster early in the time trial when they expected a flat run (unknown incline) compared to when they knew a 7 percent slope waited for them at the end. This makes sense—we often hold back a little when we expect a task to get harder and demand more of us later.

What was also interesting was how the runners responded to the unexpected slope in the unknown-incline trial. Running up a 7 percent slope is hard at any time. But running up one that you didn't expect, and didn't save something for, is even harder! These experienced runners coped by using more positive and motivational self-talk, repeating statements like "Keep going" or, for the ones who had run up the incline previously in the known-incline trial, "You've done this before." Almost amazingly, these individuals' time for the final 800-meter uphill segment didn't differ between the known- and unknown-incline trials. What did differ, however, was that participants' overall time on the unknown-incline trial was more than fourteen seconds faster than their time on the known-incline trial.

The finding of this study—that we tend to go faster if we expect something to be easier—perhaps helps to explain Salazar's strategy of telling a runner that a session will be shorter, or easier, than it ultimately proves to be. Coaches also implement strategies like these to help athletes regulate their emotional responses to pressurized situations. It's similar to the training-pool tactics implemented by Bob Bowman to help Michael Phelps cope with unexpected events in the Olympic arena. Psychologists call this tactic *pressure inurement training*.[3] It's a form of stress exposure that helps athletes practice their mental skills in a training environment and, consequently, perform better in more pressurized competitive settings.

Of course, to build resilience in this way, we not only need to be exposed to challenging events, but we also need to have the right tools at our disposal to help us through. It helped that Alvina Begay was an experienced athlete who could call on a range of tools, like chunking, focusing on process goals, and repeating motivational self-talk, to get through these challenging and unexpected training runs. But an environment—athletic or otherwise—that places high demands on us without providing an equivalent level of support, failing, for example, to teach us the mental skills to meet those challenges, can be unrelenting. Unrelenting environments can also be characterized by unhealthy competition, ridicule of those who underperform, little care for well-being, and, ultimately, feelings of isolation, stress, and burnout. In contrast, in an environment that both stretches and supports us, we can thrive and develop the tools we need to cope with the most difficult and challenging events.

"Some of the things I learned as an athlete have helped me to cope with difficult times now," Begay says. She cites her ability to keep calm and carry on in the face of uncontrollable events as key to her work in helping her Navajo community manage the COVID-19 pandemic. She was also able to be her family's bulwark when, in the thick of the pandemic, her father had a stroke and was moved to a hospital three hours from the Navajo reservation. "Running has helped me immensely in handling the unexpected," Begay says.

AFTER THE SURPRISE

We'd like to make a brief but important additional point about reacting when important events, be they in sports or everyday life, don't go as expected.

If you look at photos or video of Eliud Kipchoge winning the 2015 Berlin Marathon, you'll likely do a double take. Kipchoge went to that race with the hope of breaking what was then the world record, 2:02:57. Kipchoge also went to that race with prototypes of a Nike racing shoe. Almost immediately, things went awry in the footwear department. The insoles of both shoes came loose and started working their way above Kipchoge's feet. Kipchoge wound up running more than 20 miles of the 26.2-mile race with the insoles protruding perpendicularly to the rest of the shoes.

Kipchoge remained calm and focused despite his blistered and bloody feet. He finished in 2:04:00, a little more than a minute off the world record, but at the time his personal best. He was, of course, disappointed that defective shoes had cost him his chance at the world record. But he knew he had done the best he could on the day, and he moved on mentally. Kipchoge eventually demolished the word record, taking it down to 2:01:39 at the 2018 Berlin race, and then famously ran the first sub-2:00 marathon the following fall. (The sub-2:00 time doesn't count as the official world record because standard rules about pacing and other forms of assistance weren't followed.)

Nordic skier Kikkan Randall also once suffered an equipment mishap at the worst possible moment. She came to the 2014 Winter Olympics as the favorite in the freestyle sprint. Yet she didn't even advance past the quarterfinals.

In that qualifying race, "my skis were a bit slow," she says, meaning that she and the team's technicians didn't pick the right skis, and didn't wax them optimally, for that day's snow. "I was leading my heat at the top of the course, and I had burned a lot of energy to get in the lead and to get a bit of a gap, and when we came down the descent into the stadium, because my skis weren't as fast as others', that gap was erased," she says. "When it came to the homestretch, I didn't have that extra gear."

Randall finished five hundredths of a second out of qualifying for the semifinals. She would have to wait another four years to vie for an Olympic title.

"I was ready to win that gold medal," she says. "I knew I was capable of it, but I also knew that it's a ski race and anything can happen. I know that I gave my best effort that day. I can still walk away with good feelings from it and know that one chance where I didn't win a medal doesn't totally define me or my career."

Elite athletes are usually great at this form of equanimity because, per chapter 3, they focus on controllable actions, and they don't waste mental energy on matters they can't influence. As we saw in chapter 6, Meb Keflezighi told himself the worst marathon of his life was because of a calf cramp, so why beat himself up over the bad outcome? As did Kipchoge and Randall, he used the experience as inspiration for future competitions. Five months later, Keflezighi was the Boston Marathon champion.

Sometimes you're not going to be able to do what you know you're capable of, whether because of the weather, faulty equipment, a bad boss or unhelpful coworkers, or many other factors. If, like Randall, you can walk away knowing you gave your best, that's a win.

DON'T GET LOOPY

Just after winning the 1999 US title at 1,500 meters, Steve Holman raised his arms and tilted his head back in a gesture combining exultation, gratitude, and relief. The celebration might have seemed a bit overblown if you looked only at Holman's résumé relative to the rest of the field. He had run a 3:50 mile, while most of his competitors had bests only 1 to 3 seconds under 4:00; that's a significant difference in top-level running. Holman had twice been ranked in the top five in the world at 1,500 meters (109 meters shorter than a mile, and the distance "milers" compete at in global meets). Most of his competitors that day could better be considered national-class rather than world-class.

And yet Holman's post-race exultation made perfect sense to those familiar with his career. You'll remember from chapter 7 that Holman had felt the burden of being called "the next great American miler" since the title was bestowed on him just out of college. And indeed he was great—most of the time. No American ran faster than he did for 1,500 meters during the 1990s. He excelled in world-class races in Europe where the goal was to run as fast as possible.

"Those races were a lot like training," Holman says. "I would know what times the pacemakers would hit for the first lap, for 800 meters. Then you look at the field and roughly estimate where you should be in the pack. That was easy for me—I could just lock in and focus on the next 400-meter split and whether I was in the right position in the pack. I was really focused on the task. I was able to turn off my active mind. It's just instinct and intuition, and you're allowing your body to do what you trained it to do. It was almost like being on autopilot."

Where Holman famously struggled was at national championships, where finishing place rather than time was paramount. The top three finishers at those championships constituted the US team for the world championships (in odd-number years) or the Olympics (every four years). Those races tend to start relatively slowly, feature a lot of midrace jockeying for position, and finish with a furious sprint to grab one of the top three spots. The winning times are usually significantly slower than what Holman could run.

After starting his professional career by finishing second in the 1992 Olympic trials, Holman seemed to perform worse with each successive national championship, despite otherwise improving. Injury kept him from the 1993 national meet. In 1994, he didn't qualify for the final, but didn't worry too much about the outcome, because he was sick and there were no world championships or Olympics that year.

Things really became problematic in 1995. He came to the national meet having been ranked fifth in the world the preceding year and feeling fitter than he ever had. He wound up fifth.

"The mistake I made was, I would overthink it," he says. "I would think of every possible thing that could go wrong. It was like folks with an eating disorder—they don't think about themselves clearly. I was in unbelievable shape, but I was hypersensitive about any little thing that wasn't quite right, and anything like that could just blow up in my mind.

"I remember not feeling good during the race, and that kind of working on my mind. Instead of going on autopilot and letting my body do what it's supposed to do, I was overly focused on how tired I perceived I felt, and that worked on my confidence. There was this active conversation happening in my head that shouldn't be happening," he says.

By the 1996 Olympic trials, Holman felt trapped by his history. Media and fans (and some of his less gracious competitors) talked openly about his underperforming in national championships. For his part, "for months and months ahead of the trials, whenever I would think of that date, I would just be filled with a sense of dread," Holman says.

Spectators had reason to think he'd overcome his past. He won his quarterfinal round with an unnecessarily fast last half lap. "I figured it would look cool," Holman laughs. "It was kind of like to let everyone know I can do this, and maybe even to prove to myself I could kick like that." He also won his semifinal. "I felt great in that race," Holman says. "I didn't feel the burden I felt going into the final."

Like most championship races, the final started slowly. "I remember saying to myself, 'I feel way worse than I should at this pace.' And I thought, 'If I feel this bad when we're running this slow, when the real running starts, am I going to be able to go with them?'"

The answer: no. In third place with just more than half a lap to go, Holman didn't accelerate as the runners in front of him started their final sprint. Nor did he match strides with those who swung wide around him and passed him. He went from third to fifth to seventh and looked to be running backward as others raced away. When he finally reached the finish, he was thirteenth, ahead of only one other runner.

"It went from 'Uh-oh' to 'Oh my God' to just shame and humiliation," Holman says. "It started to sink in what was happening as it was happening. It was almost like a self-fulfilling prophecy—it was like I willed to happen what I was most worried about happening. At the end I was like, 'Well, you were right.'"

It wasn't so much that Holman didn't anticipate surprises (which is what bedeviled Ryan Hall in his 15K record attempt). It was that he knew there would be surprises, and let concern about them keep him from doing what he was physically capable of.

"The trigger for my whatever-you-want-to-call-it was that in the championship races there was more uncertainty," he says. "You don't know what to expect. Also, the stakes are higher. I was too focused on those things and I couldn't turn my mind off when I needed to in those types of races.

"It always bothered me when people would say I was a bad tactician. That really wasn't it. I knew what I needed to do strategically, and if I was in the right frame of mind, I could have done it. It was more that I couldn't consistently block other things out to put myself in a position to execute the strategy."

With the tools you've learned in this book, you might already be figuring some solutions to Holman's woes. You might reason that one way of managing uncertainty, in sport or everyday life, is to focus on those aspects of the situation that we have most control over. If so, you're absolutely right. When faced with potentially stressful events, like an Olympic trial, people who report focusing more on elements of the situation they can control usually cope more effectively.

In chapter 3, we presented a control-mapping exercise that can help you figure out what things are within your control, and what aspects of a situation lie outside of your control. But like each tool in this book, it takes practice. Every situation we encounter has different elements to consider. By using this tool, you might discover that there are more things that you can control than you realized. Bearing in mind Steve Holman's Olympic trial experiences, let's take one of these as an example.

It's probably easiest to think first of some things that you can't control. You can't control what the media, fans, or your opponents say about you before an event, for example. So, it's probably a good idea to ignore these. You also can't control the importance of a race, and as we saw in chapter 1, focusing on the outcome of an event—like whether you qualify for the Olympic games—leads to higher levels of anxiety. Finally, by definition, you also can't control whether "surprises" happen. So worrying about them is a waste of mental energy. Instead, you can plan for them and focus on how you might respond to them. This is important, since when you focus on controllable responses, uncontrollable surprises become less of a concern.

Thinking of the factors you can't control might highlight the things you can control. By using tools like breathing and grounding techniques (chapter 2), reappraising the situation, reappraising your thoughts and emotional responses (as by reframing anxiety as excitement), and staying in the moment (chapter 3), you can control how you think and feel in a potentially stressful situation. You can shift your viewpoint, going from seeing an event as a threat to eyeing it as a challenge. In other words, by applying the right mental tools, you can influence your mental state and, subsequently, how you think and feel. By practicing under simulated pressure, and responding with calmness and composure during training, you can also create a template for how you might respond to unexpected events in high-pressure situations.

But even with an effective mental tool kit, and extensive planning and preparation, it's important to remember that surprises can happen. For these, other strategies can be effective. Being able to accept that unexpected things can happen is important to managing our mindset. Sometimes adopting a "fuck it" attitude, as self-diagnosed overthinker Steve Kerr did during his NBA career, can be important to help overcome an endless loop of debilitating thoughts and irrelevant distractions.

After his disastrous Olympic trials race in 1996, Holman started seeing a sport psychologist. The terms used back then were a little different from today, but much of what Holman did meshes with current recommendations.

"I didn't need to get worked up for big races—I was on the far end of overstimulation," Holman says. "I needed the opposite. So one thing we did was general anxiety management—meditation techniques, deep-breathing exercises, learning how to calm myself."

Holman also focused on managing negative thoughts. "There was a lot of work on reframing—when a negative thought comes up, how do you stop it and replace it with a positive thought?" he says. Relatedly, Holman did a lot of visualization, going through important races in his head and using positive experiences as a template.

"I would picture a great race I had in Europe, or a great workout," Holman says. "I would think about how I felt and what I thought in those, and try to get that feeling in my body. Then I would think about an upcoming championship race, and try to get that same mindset and apply it to that race. I was both relaxing myself and creating a positive mindset going into the race.

"In the 1999 championship, I feel like I conquered it."

No one who had followed Holman's career would disagree.

CHAPTER 10

Perceived Effort
and Perseverance

*What to Do When Things Feel
Harder Than They Should*

———

THINK BACK TO A WORKOUT or time at work when things just clicked. You felt a sense of mastery, that your physical and mental capabilities perfectly matched the demands of the situation. In chapter 3, we looked at these "in-the-zone" moments and the factors that go into achieving a state of flow.

Now think back to the bulk of your workouts or work over the past few weeks. Most were probably what we might call "good-enough" days—you weren't firing on all cylinders, and you may have used a few of this book's mental tools to help yourself along, but things weren't unduly challenging. These good-enough days were what we had in mind in chapter 8 when we discussed one way to keep working toward your goals: recalling previous times when you felt less than great but forged ahead with the day's demands and did just fine.

Now think about some really tough days. For no apparent reason, you struggled to hit your usual pace or distance while working out. Or typical tasks at work required much more concentration, with worse results, than usual. By definition, you don't face this situation every day. (If you do, it's time to rethink what constitutes "normal"!) But their relative infrequency doesn't make these days any easier. In this chapter, we'll look at several tools for carrying on when things feel harder than they should.

SHIFTING STANDARDS

Meb Keflezighi began 2014 with a surprisingly good performance at the Houston Half Marathon. He went to the race in part to fulfill an obligation to his shoe sponsor, Skechers, which was also a major sponsor of the event. Keflezighi wound up winning the national half marathon championship in 61:23, only 23 seconds slower than his five-year-old personal best. Even the ever-optimistic Keflezighi was a little amazed at such a strong performance two months after the slowest marathon of his life. He left Houston fired up for what he thought would be his last run at the Boston Marathon.

Keflezighi was superb at aiming high while remaining grounded in reality. He would turn thirty-nine a few weeks after running Boston in April. His body didn't bounce back from long runs and hard workouts as it had only five years earlier, when he won the New York City Marathon, and certainly not as it had a decade earlier, when he placed second in the Olympic marathon. One major adjustment he made in his Boston preparation was to shift from a seven-day to a nine-day training cycle. Instead of fitting a long run and two hard workouts into each calendar week, Keflezighi followed each of those key sessions with two recovery days of easier running.

But, as anyone who has trained hard in their late thirties could have predicted, Keflezighi still had many difficult days, made all the more difficult by their randomness. He would, for example, start to do a series of one-mile repeats at his half marathon race pace and struggle from the start to hit his desired times. A master at motivating himself under duress, Keflezighi described his approach to these situations in his book *Meb for Mortals*:

> If I'm doing mile repeats and I'm getting a little slower on each one, I'll focus on my average for the session. So instead of thinking, "I started at 4:35, then ran 4:38, then 4:41; this is just getting worse and worse," I'll tell myself, "You're averaging 4:38. Now how close to that can you get on this next one?"[1]

Keflezighi's flexible approach to goal setting might sound familiar. It also highlights the benefits of open goals, which we introduced in chapter 1 ("How Good Can I Get?"). Adapting your goals to your current reality is a key strategy for when things feel harder than they should. After retiring from world-class rowing in 2016, Brianna Stubbs became an accomplished triathlete who twice qualified for the Half Ironman world championship. She mostly works out by herself in her new sport, in contrast to the team practices that marked much of her rowing career. She also trains around a full-time work schedule as a lead scientist at the Buck Institute for Research on Aging just north of San Francisco. Translation: Stubbs is no stranger to motivating herself on harder-than-they-should-be days.

"One thing that has really helped me—and I know it sounds like a silly trope—is if you're having a 3-out-of-10 day, make it a 3-out-of-3 day," she says. "It's like being at peace with the fact that you can't be at 100 percent all of the time, and doing what you can with the energy level you have and with what the conditions are."

Stubbs thinks this strategy not only helps on any given day but also contributes to future sucess.

"I've never stopped a hard workout," she says. "I think that's a dangerous habit, because once you see people start to bail, then it becomes easy to do that again. I think it's better to reframe things—that 3-out-of-3 or 7-out-of-7 mentality. So if I'm having a hard day on the bike, I'll think, 'I can't hold the 200 watts I'm trying to hold right now, so I'm going to hold 185 as long as I can.' It's being able on the fly to set targets that still keep you working and motivated."

TALK TO YOURSELF ABOUT CHUNKS

Situations that feel harder than they should are also a prime opportunity to combine two tools we described in this book's first section: chunking, from chapter 1, and motivational self-talk, from chapter 4. Chunking, you'll recall, entails breaking a seemingly overwhelming task into smaller, manageable bits and focusing on only one of those bits at a time. Here's how Olympic ski champion Kikkan Randall describes her simultaneous use of those techniques:

"One thing that really helped me was making goals on the fly, to keep myself focused on the moment," she says. "So this is where you're in a 30[-kilometer] race and you're 1 [kilometer] into it and the pace already feels ridiculously hard and you're like, 'How can I possibly keep this up?' That's when you say, 'OK, don't think about 30K at once. Let's think about how to ski this next K. Let's see if you can hang with this group until the 5K mark.' Or, 'Look at the top of that hill, let's just get there.' And then when you come to the top of the hill, you come up with the next thing.

That was really powerful—to give my mind little things to focus on in the midst of this longer time or distance."

Randall also combined self-talk with other key tools, reappraisal (chapter 2) and mindful acceptance (chapter 3), to help herself view what might be an incapacitating situation as something more manageable.

"Every thought that comes into your mind, you have a choice of how you acknowledge that," she says. "It's important to acknowledge every thought, but our human nature tends to focus on the negative, like, 'Oh man, this pace is really hard,' or 'Oh man, these competitors look really good,' or 'Oh man, conditions look tough today.'

"Acknowledge that thought, but always try to reframe it in a positive direction, like, 'Yeah, my competition's looking tough today, but you've hung with them before, you've prepared well, you're ready for this.' Or, 'OK, they're better than you, let's see what it's like to hang with them and get a feel for that pace.' Or, 'The weather conditions are horrible today. Well, good thing you did that training session two weeks ago in those horrible conditions, because now you're ready to face the conditions in today's race.'"

As we saw in chapter 4, addressing yourself as "you" rather than "I" is often more effective in these dig-deep situations ("who are you talking to?" tool). Randall says about her self-talk, "I take on this third-person cheerleader-personality role. It's kind of coaching me, encouraging me. It's like the mind that's acknowledging the thought is me. Then there's the negative voice that wants to be the Debbie Downer. And then there's the other voice that's like, 'Nope, nope, you can do this, you're prepared to do this.'"

RECALL YOUR PAST MASTERY

Note how in her reframing self-talk, Randall reminded herself of having overcome bad weather previously. Recalling previous incidents of prevailing—or at least persevering—can be a powerful tool when things feel harder than they should.

Meb Keflezighi drew on such memories during the 2014 Boston Marathon. In his previous eighteen marathons, he had run with the lead pack or a chase pack for as long as possible. Doing so helped him conserve physical and mental energy and was usually necessary to place as high as possible. (You don't win a major marathon by letting ten world-class runners build a big lead over you.) But things played out differently that year in Boston. At around the 5-mile mark, Keflezighi's momentum carried him into a slight lead. He realized the fourteen runners in the field with faster personal bests were trying to keep the early pace slow. Keflezighi, who was always motivated by running fast as well as placing high, felt he was capable of improving his personal record that day, and didn't want to waste the opportunity. So rather than easing back into the pack, he forged ahead. One other runner, Josphat Boit, went with him, but fell back a few miles later. By the 10-mile mark, Keflezighi was the solo leader of the world's most famous marathon, on a day when the race was receiving extraordinary attention because of the bombings the year before, and he still had 16 miles to run.

Rather than think, "I've never been in this situation before, what am I going to do?" Keflezighi thought about his training. He had done almost all his running by himself the previous few years. He told himself he was used to doing solo 10- or 15-mile runs at his marathon race pace, and that if he could complete those challenging workouts solo in the midst of heavy training, surely he could now keep running that pace in what had become the most important race of his life.

As we learned in chapter 5, recalling past moments like these can have a powerful impact on our belief that we can do what we need to do to perform at our best. Our previous accomplishments are our strongest source to fuel this self-belief.

Moreover, how we perceive these past accomplishments is also important. If Keflezighi had reflected that he had maintained his race-pace training only because he had drafted behind a training partner, or because he had completed each run on well-rested legs, then recalling his past accomplishments might not have changed his beliefs much during those doubt-filled moments in Boston. Attributing those training efforts to his own hard work, however, and reflecting that he had maintained his marathon race pace despite feeling fatigued from a heavy training schedule, provided a boost to his in-the-moment beliefs of what he was capable of over the final 16 miles of the race.

The strategies used by Keflezighi, Randall, and Stubbs also serve as a useful reminder of the different "in-the-zone" states we introduced in chapter 3. To achieve peak performances, athletes don't always enter a state of flow. Sometimes, when the outcome is on the line, athletes need to make their best performance happen. These clutch performances are achieved when athletes make a conscious effort to reach a performance target and do so by using mental tools that best fit their needs in the moment. As

Keflezighi, Randall, and Stubbs highlight, these techniques can include effective goal setting, mindful acceptance, reappraisal, motivational self-talk, and reminders of previous accomplishments to boost self-belief.

Drawing on past athletic mastery can also help during tough times outside of sports. Kikkan Randall regularly leaned on her ski-racing days during her long weeks of chemotherapy for breast cancer.

"On the really tough days, when I wasn't feeling good," she says, "I tried to remind myself of all the times I felt that way when I was ski racing and going through an illness or injury, and how those days feel like the longest ever, but you're hopeful that tomorrow will be better. [Knowing] at some point I'll feel better again, being that cheerleader, reminding myself of that, reminding myself to get through it one day at a time."

CHANGE YOUR PERCEPTIONS

The Newton fire station sits a little past the 17-mile mark of the Boston Marathon. It's the site of the last turn on the course until the final mile. As Meb Keflezighi made the turn in the 2014 race, he took a long look back. He saw no other runners. The lead he'd seized forty-five minutes earlier had grown. He didn't know how big his lead was, but then again, the chase pack didn't know how far ahead he was. Keflezighi decided to push hard the next 4 miles over the famed Newton hills to keep himself out of sight, and hopefully out of mind, of his pursuers.

The road surface of the Newton hills is usually peppered with temporary motivation phrases like YOU GOT THIS! on race day. In 2014, the words BOSTON STRONG were also visible on and along the course. Although intensely focused on executing his race strategy, Keflezighi couldn't help noticing the year's special messages. He didn't experience them as unhelpful distractions. Rather, he drew strength from them, just as he did from having written the names of the bombing's four fatalities on his race bib. These cues reminded him this wasn't just another marathon. It was a race he wanted to win to reclaim the event from the horrors of the previous year.

The always-knowledgeable Boston crowd knew the significance of Keflezighi's quest. Easily identified by the name MEB on his bib, he was cheered up and over the Newton hills. Rather than ignoring the boisterous crowd, Keflezighi used it to his advantage. Chants of "USA! USA!" bolstered his determination to win as an American. Keflezighi occasionally acknowledged the crowd with a thumbs-up or fist pump. A biomechanical engineer might have told Keflezighi not to waste precious energy with such gestures. A sport psychologist, however, might have realized Keflezighi knew exactly what he was doing.

Keflezighi's experience of drawing inspiration from the crowd, and benefiting from the motivational support they provided, highlights two of the most important variables that can influence the performance of endurance athletes.

One of the limiting factors to endurance performance is how hard we perceive an activity to be. We generally keep going until a task feels harder than we're willing to push.

Two strategies can change this threshold and, with it, our performance. One is to increase our levels of motivation or, more accurately, the quality of our motivation and, in doing so, increase how hard we're willing to push.

Relatively weak forms of motivation include doing things because we expect a reward—like a medal—and doing things because we would feel guilty if we didn't. The highest quality of motivation comes when we're driven to do tasks that we find intrinsically interesting and enjoyable, or that are personally important to us and based on our values.[2] This latter form of motivation helps to explain why so many of us run marathons or donate time and money to charities that hold meaning for us.[3] Doing something hard because helping to make life better for others is important to us can be a powerful motivator.

Reminders of why we're doing something are also important. For Keflezighi, being the first American man to win the Boston Marathon since 1983, and doing so the year after the bombings, was the most meaningful goal he'd set in his career. Seeing the "Boston Strong" messages along the course proved a powerful reminder of that motivation at a critical stage of the race.

The second strategy to increase how hard we're willing to push is to use mental techniques to make a task feel easier. In chapters 3 and 4 we explored many of these techniques. They include distracting ourselves from the activity we're completing ("The Case for Tuning Out," chapter 3) and not focusing excessively on bodily sensations like muscle soreness or breathing ("The Case for Tuning In," chapter 3). Using motivational and challenge-based self-talk (chapter 4) can also make an endurance task feel easier and, as a result, improve performance. Given this, it's easy to imagine the impact of the vociferous Boston crowd, not only on Keflezighi's motivation but also on his perception of effort over the challenging Newton hills.

ATHLETES AT WORK

Research has also shown that while athletes and sedentary people have similar pain thresholds, athletes score much higher on tests of pain tolerance. That is, if athletes and sedentary people were to participate in a study involving submerging a hand in ice water, both groups would say after about the same amount of time that their hands hurt; that's pain threshold. But once their hands started hurting, athletes would keep their hands in the ice water for significantly longer than sedentary people; that's pain tolerance.

At least one study has suggested that athletes' greater tolerance isn't inherent and doesn't explain why they became athletes in the first place. When researchers took a group of sedentary people and had half of them begin a modest exercise program of thrice-weekly thirty-minute bike rides, the new athletes had greater pain tolerance at the end of the study than they had at the beginning, while the participants who remained sedentary were no better. Regular workouts, it seems, build our ability to put up with discomfort, and that ability appears to apply even to situations we don't specifically encounter in our workouts.

There's a psychological parallel to these findings on pain threshold and pain tolerance. Here the nemesis isn't physical pain but mental strain. Athletes have regular experience with persevering through discomfort to reach a goal. The mental tools they use to navigate those difficult times are available to them in other settings, including the workplace, perhaps to a greater degree than they are to their sedentary colleagues.

That was certainly an observation made by Steve Holman and Brianna Stubbs early in their post-sport professional careers. Both spent much of their youth and early adulthood surrounded almost entirely by other world-class athletes. Both took on leadership roles soon after joining "the real world." Both have found that drawing on trying athletic times helps them get themselves and the people they manage through tough stretches at work.

"The term that's used now in business is a *growth mind-set*," Holman says. "Athletes have had this for years, but we didn't call it that back in the day. The way to approach things to maximize success is to focus on what's possible as opposed to what's wrong or what you can't do. You have to be really creative and resourceful to give yourself confidence that you can achieve whatever goal you have or address whatever the issue is.

"I feel that has helped me as a leader because if something blows up, I don't think, 'This is a disaster,' or I'm not looking to point fingers, or I'm not making sure people don't perceive it as my fault. Instead, I immediately click onto, 'What are the things we can latch on that gives us some hope that there's a resolution? How do we solve this problem?'

"I definitely think that's related to the athletic mindset. If you think about it, if you say something like, 'I'm going to make the Olympic team,' that's just an audacious, bizarre statement. You have to have some reservoir of optimism and positivity that makes you believe you can actually do that. I think the same thing at work is, 'Yeah, we run into challenges, but there's no challenge that's so impossible that we can't figure out a way to deal with it.'"

Stubbs says, "You learn this through sport—stuff doesn't go perfectly all the time. You learn that there are ups and downs and injuries as well as dazzling high points. You have to wholeheartedly embrace both parts of that to get to the best experience. In the real world, you have to give people permission to have highs and lows rather than just deliver 'medium' all the time."

Holman, who, twenty years after retiring from professional track, still runs or cycles most days, says, "I feel like I'm more resilient than the average person at work. You have to be resilient as an athlete. You're not going to win every race, you're not always going to be successful, you're going to have tough days. You have to be able to put that behind you and focus on what you need to do next."

A FINAL WORD ON CHALLENGING TIMES

One of the key things we hope you'll take away from this book is that you can always improve your think-like-an-athlete skills. Regular work in this area leads to a greater pool of psychological resources to call on, in the same way that regular work in the gym leads to greater physical strength. As Kikkan Randall says about decades of working on positive self-talk, "I found that with practice I got better at it, and that is a skill that has helped me in all aspects of my life."

As we've seen, Randall succeeded in skiing thanks in part to these skills. She then successfully applied them to better navigate being treated for aggressive breast cancer. The latter, of course, is of far greater importance than sports in the grand scheme of things. Regardless of the particulars of our most trying days, we can all master the approach Randall took while fighting cancer.

"There are a lot of things that don't always go your way," she says. "You don't know what's going to happen, so just do the best with what you can. And why not imagine that things can go well? You're better off making it through the tough days than to always go, 'Oh my God, the cancer's coming back, I may not make it.'

"The one thing you can choose is your mindset, and I think that's really powerful."

CHAPTER 11

Stop the Stopping

How to Keep Going When the Desire
to Quit Feels Overwhelming

———

THE KERRY WAY ULTRA is the longest and most difficult running event in Ireland. Setting out at 6:00 AM on a Friday, participants face a nonstop 120-mile course with almost 18,500 feet of elevation gain, traversing the laneways, trails, forests, and muddy mountain passes parallel to Ireland's scenic Ring of Kerry route.

To qualify, entrants are required to have completed at least two marathons or one 50-mile race in the preceding twelve months. Having competed in the Marathon des Sables in 2012 and Ireland's twenty-four-hour championships in 2013, Noel headed into the 2014 Kerry Way Ultra feeling confident that his previous experiences—not to mention insights from his professional life—would help him deal with any challenge the race could throw at him. And yet . . .

Years later, Noel still calls the event the hardest of his life. It was the rare race in which he repeatedly encountered the urge to quit. He wasn't alone in that desire; in the race's first eight years, 47 percent of participants exited the event with a DNF (runnerese for "did not finish") beside their name.

For Noel, the urge to abandon came at many points during the race. The first coincided with a bout of nausea and stomach cramps after six hours, a legacy from days before the race when Noel—who is gluten-intolerant—had unwittingly eaten some food contaminated with gluten. The symptoms were mild, but sufficient to affect his race-day nutrition throughout the event. As the day grew warmer, Noel's inner voice whispered softly, "Maybe it's not safe to keep going?"

But Noel had experienced this voice before. He countered it by reminding himself that he could do this ("self-talk" tool, chapter 4) and had been through long, grinding races before ("previous accomplishments" tool, chapter 5). Traversing some of the most scenic parts of the route, and deliberately focusing his attention on these views ("The Case for Tuning Out," chapter 3), also helped Noel stay calm, mentally pass the time, and keep his mind off his many mounting physical woes.

A second, stronger urge to quit came after the race's midpoint, on the long and winding mountain path that led to the seaside village of Waterville. For Noel, who was feeling physically and mentally exhausted after 60 miles and fourteen hours of running (or shuffling), the impending nightfall and the prospect of another 60 miles ahead was daunting. The inner voice grew louder as darkness descended. "I really should be going to sleep now, and I don't want to be tired for work next week. It's best to stop now. I've done well to get this far!"

If Noel is honest, he listened for a while! Fortunately, Noel's parents had decided to meet him in the village and brought with them some Coke, fruit yogurt, and a change of footwear. They sat together for a while on a bench in the town square, underneath the shadow cast by a statue of one of Noel's childhood sporting heroes, former Gaelic football player and coach Mick O'Dwyer. The welcome rest, some sustenance, and the distraction afforded by a conversation provided a brief respite from thoughts about stopping.

The rest stop also gave Noel an opportunity to express, rather than suppress, his feelings and chat through his thoughts ("How Can I Regulate My Emotions?," chapter 2). It helped to strengthen his resolve, and with a reminder that "you can do this" ("Who Are You Talking To?," chapter 4), he decided to venture onward, determined to get to the next checkpoint at least! ("chunk it" tool, chapter 1.)

Occasional urges to abandon the race recurred throughout the night. One memorable occasion came just after 2:00 AM, twenty hours into the race. Poor pre-race planning meant Noel's headlamp battery died on a section of the route overlooking the village of Sneem, not far from where his brother lived. Feeling tired and miserable, and guided only by the faint beam of his phone, Noel heard his inner voice begin to shout. "It's the middle of the night, I feel miserable, and this is utter madness! What are you doing on this mountain in the darkness? Maybe you should call your brother and ask him to pick you up in his car?"

But strange things happen in the middle of the night on a mountain in Kerry. Noel stumbled, figuratively and literally, into the 1991 world mountain running champion, John Lenihan, who appeared out of the darkness with a pen and clipboard in hand, ticking off participants who passed through to ensure they made it safely off the mountain. Thoughts of "I feel miserable" were replaced by thoughts of

"Wow, that was John Lenihan! And he's prepared to spend all night on this mountain to ensure everyone gets home safely. Maybe you should keep going!"

Noel's spirits were further lifted shortly afterward when he met his brother—with spare batteries in hand—just before he entered the village. His brother's encouragement—coupled with a supportive phone call from his wife, Holly—lifted the gloom and helped to keep Noel motivated to continue. As we learned in chapter 2, reflecting on the positive things in our lives, like things our family has done for us, and expressing gratitude for them, can benefit how we feel ("Write About It" and gratitude techniques, chapter 2). It certainly helped Noel to keep going when he wasn't sure he could.

Despite these positive moments, the final thirteen hours of shuffling were incredibly tough. At one point just after dawn, Noel almost fell asleep as he rested momentarily—hands on knees—in a woodland trail. But by constantly reminding himself, "I can do this" ("self-talk" tool, chapter 4), and "This too will pass" ("think again" tool, chapter 2), and acknowledging that he did want to stop, but mindfully accepting that those thoughts were inevitable at this point of the race ("Tuning In to the Present Moment," chapter 3), Noel got through each moment of doubt.

Noel eventually finished the race in thirty-three hours and forty-seven minutes. It took him every trick in the book—this book—to get there.

DEFEATING THE DNF DESIRE

Wanting to quit usually happens when we're in the second half of a difficult undertaking and ridding ourselves of mental and physical duress seems paramount. Above and below, you'll find several keys to countering that urge.

Perhaps the most important point to keep in mind is this: Almost everybody thinks about quitting at some point. Having those thoughts doesn't make you a weak person or a failure. Meb Keflezighi wanted to drop out of each of the twenty-six marathons he ran as a professional—including the three he won!

He did so only once, in the 2007 London Marathon, when his right Achilles tendon became acutely painful and he started to slow dramatically in the fourteenth mile. Keflezighi reasoned that running another 12 miles on the injury could have long-term consequences that wouldn't be justified by the poor time he seemed destined to finish in. He stepped off the course in the sixteenth mile.

In his twenty-five other pro marathons, Keflezighi conquered the DNF desire. His success in doing so came in part from previous experience, in two ways. First, he knew the urge would come, so when it did, it wasn't a surprise; he had a plan for countering it. Second, each time that he persisted, he built self-confidence and learned techniques that would help him navigate the same thoughts in his next marathon.

Many of the tools that Keflezighi and other successful athletes use to stay the course are similar to those we recommended in the previous chapter. There, the goal was to keep yourself from lessening your effort when things feel harder than they should. Of course, quitting is the ultimate act of lessening your effort. How to deploy those tools can be a little different when you're using them to stop yourself from stopping.

As Noel's experience during the 2014 Kerry Way Ultra suggests, the solutions often depend on the situation you find yourself in. So, rather than having any hard-and-fast rules about which procedures to use, building your mental tool kit by practicing the techniques we present in this book means you have a range of tools at your disposal. You can then flexibly use those tools to dig yourself out of goal-achievement difficulties whenever and wherever you experience them.

Again, the key point is not that we avoid thoughts of stopping or quitting in the first place. As we learned in chapter 4 ("Changing the Story: How Self-Talk Training Works for Athletes")—and as Keflezighi's marathon career reminds us—psychological crises and moments of doubt happen to even the most experienced of athletes. Instead of expecting yourself to eliminate these inner voices, the best approach is to have refined a range of effective ways to respond to them each time they do arise.

WHEN QUITTING IS WINNING

Another important big-picture point: Sometimes stopping is the right choice. If you crash and break a collarbone during the cycling portion of a triathlon, soldiering on for the rest of the ride and the subsequent run probably isn't in your best long-term interest. In athletic events, continuing to compete despite a form-altering injury or some other severe bodily woe isn't heroic or character building; it's a mistake.

Some athletes also disengage from a task if they view it as pointless to continue. In cycling stage races such as the Tour de France, breakaway riders will slow and wait to be caught if they realize that continuing in their attempt is a waste of energy and unlikely to result in a stage victory. Best to conserve resources for another attempt on a subsequent day!

A number of psychological processes are relevant to deciding whether to disengage from a goal. One is how personally meaningful or enjoyable the challenge of pursuing a goal is. The findings of a two-part study led by Nikos Ntoumanis, PhD, of the University of Birmingham in the UK, emphasize this point.[1]

In part one of the study, the research team asked a group of sixty-six athletes to complete an eight-minute cycling trial during which they were given a distance goal to achieve. Participants were also asked to rate the quality of their motives to achieve the goal. These motives ranged from weaker, controlled forms of motivation, such as pursuing the distance goal "because I feel I am expected to," to higher-quality, autonomous forms of motivation, such as striving to achieve the distance "because of the enjoyment or challenge the pursuit of the goal provides."

During the trial, despite their best efforts, the participants were provided with deceptive feedback that led them to believe that their goal was unattainable. The researchers were interested to know whether participants would abandon their goal and give up completely, or mentally reengage with alternative goals—ones they developed on the fly—and continue their efforts.

Intriguingly, the researchers found that individuals who held more autonomous forms of motivation—that is, who were chasing the distance goal because they enjoyed the challenge and perceived it as personally meaningful—had more trouble giving up on the initial goal because they had invested more psychological resources and physical effort into it. No such relationship existed for participants with lower-quality, controlled forms of motivation. In addition, whereas lower-quality motivation was also unrelated to the decision to chase an alternative goal, those with higher-quality motives were more likely to mentally reengage in alternative goals than they were to give up completely. This is similar to the "shifting standards" strategy Meb Keflezighi described using in chapter 10 to get through mile-repeat training sessions that felt harder than they should.

To further investigate this reengagement process, in part two of the study researchers gave a different group of eighty-six participants the opportunity to reengage in an alternative goal on a rowing ergometer whenever they realized the eight-minute cycling goal had become unattainable. Participants had three choices in this trial: persist futilely on the cycling task; disengage from cycling once they realized their goal was unattainable and reengage in a different goal on a rowing ergometer for the remainder of the eight-minute session; or give up and abandon the trial completely.

As in part one of the study, participants who were motivated by the thrill of the chase found it more difficult to disengage from the cycling task both behaviorally and mentally. In other words, they were more likely to persist in a futile chase, and were also more likely to ruminate over their goal failure. But these individuals were also more likely to reengage with a different goal on the rowing ergometer than give up completely.

This suggests that we find it much harder to give up on an unattainable goal that we find interesting, enjoyable, or personally meaningful. But how much we've already invested in pursuit of the goal is also important. When the researchers dug deeper into the data, they noticed that the timing of participants' realization that their goal was unattainable was related to goal-abandonment decisions. The earlier they had this realization, the easier it was for them to disengage from the cycling goal and reengage with the alternative rowing goal. And this highlights the key challenge we face in pursuing any demanding goal. It's not always easy to know whether difficulties in goal striving can be overcome with greater effort and persistence, or should be taken as a warning of impending failure. If the latter is the case, then knowing when to abandon the chase is key.

An extreme version of effective goal disengagement came in the 1996 Zurich Weltklasse track meet. With one lap to go, Daniel Komen of Kenya and Haile Gebrselassie of Ethiopia were on pace to break Gebrselassie's 5,000-meter world record. Gebrselassie had won the Olympic 10,000-meter title two weeks earlier. Komen hadn't run in the Olympics and was fresher. As Komen started his final push, Gebrselassie couldn't keep up, and settled into a jog with less than 150 meters to go.

What looked like inexplicable wimpiness on the part of one of the greatest distance runners in history was actually a shrewd move. Gebrselassie knew his body well enough to know he wouldn't beat Komen. He also knew that continuing to challenge Komen would spur his rival to a faster time. On his own, Komen didn't find the necessary extra gear, and missed Gebrselassie's record by seven tenths of a second. In that sense, Gebrselassie "won" by giving up, because the world record remained his.

There are also longer-term projects in which not doggedly seeing things through is the right choice. Of this book's two authors, only Noel has a PhD. After getting his master's degree, Scott began what turned out to be one of the briefest stints as a PhD candidate in US education history. He quit during the first semester when he realized he wasn't sufficiently motivated by the PhD goal to invest several more years of school and tens of thousands of dollars.

In doing so, he avoided what economists call the *sunk-cost fallacy*. That's the tendency to continue doing something primarily because of the time or money already spent on it. If you've ever sat through the second half of a movie you're not enjoying rather than leave the theater because exiting would be "wasting" the ticket price, you've fallen prey to the sunk-cost fallacy. Whether you stay or go, you've already paid for the ticket, so that shouldn't figure into decisions about how to spend the time remaining in the movie.

In Scott's case, cutting his losses and quitting the PhD program opened the door to other professional avenues. There are also scenarios where leaving an endeavor but returning to it later is the right choice. Through the third of her six rounds of chemotherapy for breast cancer, Olympic ski champion Kikkan Randall remained committed to her pre-diagnosis goal of running that fall's New York City Marathon. "I knew I wasn't going to be able to run a personal best, but to say I'm going through chemo and ran a marathon would be a cool story," she says.

But by her fourth round of treatment, the cumulative toll on her body was too much. "I realized I could probably gut my way through it but doing so wouldn't be the smartest thing," Randall says. Instead, she went to New York to cheer on a teammate who was running the marathon. On race morning, Randall slogged through a forty-five-minute run that confirmed the wisdom of skipping that year's race. She returned the following year, 2019, once her treatment was over, and ran 2:55, which was as fast as she thought she could run pre-cancer. Randall's postponement strategy is also valid if you have a significant injury or more mundane but sustained interruptions during the buildup to a key goal.

WHEN TO HOLD, WHEN TO FOLD

Knowing when to remain focused and not withdraw your effort too quickly, and when to disengage from an ultimately futile goal, can be difficult. Clearly, we can't provide one-size-fits-all advice to direct your decision-making process. But we can provide you with a tool that will help. It's called *decisional balance*[2] and is regularly used by psychologists to help people resolve ambivalence by considering their own arguments for and against a course of action.[3] By guiding us through this process, decisional balance can help us make key life decisions, including whether we should remain committed to a goal, abandon our attempt, or engage our efforts in an alternative, worthwhile goal.

Many of us complete a decisional balance in our heads when weighing the pros and cons of a situation. We do it for short-term, in-the-moment decisions, like Haile Gebrselassie's decision to quit during the final lap in the 1996 Weltklasse meet. We also do it for longer-term and potentially life-changing decisions, like Kikkan Randall's decision to prioritize her cancer treatment over her goal of running the 2018 New York City Marathon. Although completing a mental decisional balance is helpful, taking some time to write down all considerations can help you make a more balanced and considered judgment.

To complete a decisional balance, divide a page into four quadrants, just as in the diagram below. List all the benefits of quitting that you can think of in the first quadrant, and all the costs of quitting in the second. Benefits of quitting might include more time to dedicate to other goals or aspects of your life, like family, for example. Costs of quitting might include the frustration or disappointment you expect to feel when giving up a long-held ambition. It doesn't matter how big or inconsequential each of these pros and cons is; write them all down. What's important is that you consider each as part of your decision-making process.

In the third quadrant, list all the benefits of keeping going. In the final quadrant, list all the costs of persevering. Those benefits might be that you experience a sense of satisfaction and gain some reward when you achieve your goal. Costs of keeping going could include a reduction in your overall health and well-being, and that striving for one goal—as Kikkan Randall realized—can affect your ability to pursue other important life goals. The final decision comes when you weigh up all the benefits and costs of each course of action.

Decisional Balance

Benefits of Quitting	Costs of Quitting
Benefits of Keeping Going	Costs of Keeping Going

Completing a decisional balance can result in a number of different outcomes. An objective cost-benefit analysis can mean you avoid the all-consuming chase of an unattainable goal when the costs of continuing outweigh the benefits.[4] But it can also reaffirm your commitment to an achievable goal and help you overcome a difficult and challenging moment.[5] In doing so, you avoid quitting too early and increase your likelihood of achieving your goal if it can be successfully completed.

DRAWING ON RESILIENCE

We've talked a lot in this book about the resilience of athletes. As we learned in chapter 6, psychological resilience—our capacity to bounce back or keep going and maintain our performance, functioning, and well-being despite the challenges we face—isn't a quality we "have" so much as one we develop by using the mental techniques at our disposal. The ability to keep moving forward despite significant challenges underlies much success in sport and everyday life. It can also make us a source of strength and self-belief to others who might be more likely to give up during trying times ("learn from others" tool, chapter 5).

No time in recent collective memory was more trying than the COVID-19 pandemic. Many athletes have said that the psychological skills they learned through sport were key to surviving the long months of altered life. Techniques such as chunking time (chapter 1), focusing on things under their control and accepting events that were uncontrollable (chapter 3), adjusting goals on the go (chapter 10), maintaining positive self-talk (chapter 4), and many others from this book helped those who think like an athlete to continue functioning rather than give in to despair.

Alvina Begay, whom we met in chapter 9, drew on her decades of ambitious running to help herself, her family, and her community during the pandemic. A two-time Olympic marathon trials qualifier with a best of 2:37 in the event, Begay lives on the Navajo Nation, a Native American reservation that encompasses northeastern Arizona, southeastern Utah, and northwestern New Mexico. The area was among the hardest hit in the United States by the pandemic, with high caseloads and hundreds of deaths.

Begay works as a dietitian in a dialysis center on the reservation. She earned a nursing degree a few months before the pandemic hit. (Her mother is the director of nursing at another Navajo health care facility.) She combined her medical education with her running background to rally her people when she felt they were ready to give up. Because of her running renown and social media following, Begay says, "I have a platform, and I was determined to use it to spread positive messages."

The challenges were many. Lack of access to running water, affecting about one third of the Navajo Nation's population of 170,000, makes regular handwashing unlikely. Those without running water often shower and do dishes and laundry at a family member's house, thereby increasing the chance of community virus spread. Diabetes and obesity are rampant in the community; Begay attributes that in part to canned goods and fast food being many people's main food options. Poor underlying health increased the severity of illness once people contracted COVID-19.

Cultural practices also worked against the Navajo. "Shaking someone's hand as a formal greeting is deeply ingrained," Begay says. It is typical for large families to live in close quarters, partly out of economic necessity but also because kinship ties are so important. "It's normal to visit your aunts and grandmas on a daily basis," Begay says, "and all of a sudden they're being told, 'Stay at home, don't shake hands.'"

Her attempts to share basic public-health messages were also hindered by a certain overconfidence. "A lot of the population, especially the elderly, have the attitude, 'We've already overcome so much, our ancestors have overcome so much, we're going to get through this,'" Begay says, "and because they have that attitude, some of them don't take the precautions seriously."

Like an athlete reframing a negative thought into something self-motivating, Begay reminded her community that their ancestors overcame so much by adhering to the best of their cultural traditions. That includes running.

"I kept going back to the stories I was raised with," she says. "We were taught about the benefits of getting up early and running toward the east every morning, the importance of taking care of your body and mind. Our teachings are about learning to be strong and that, when you do difficult things, you're preparing yourself to handle difficult situations."

Begay's overarching message: Don't quit. Don't give up on the proven measures to slow the spread of the virus. After all the community has been through, don't let this challenge be the one that leads to resignation. That message became all the more important when her father had a stroke early in the pandemic and was hospitalized hours away.

"When that double hit of COVID and my father came, some of the things I learned as an athlete were what got me through and helped me help my family," Begay says. "As an athlete, you're used to taking hits and still getting up and moving on no matter how hard things are. I would tell them, 'Things are really shitty right now, but we're OK, there are still so many things to be grateful for. Dad made some progress today. Let's take that little win and move forward to tomorrow.'"

CHAPTER 12

Finish Strong

*How to Keep Pushing in
the Final Stretch*

———

MOLLY HUDDLE POWERED into the final lap of the 2015 world championship 10,000-meter run with one goal: to put herself in the best position possible to win her first medal in a global meet. Huddle knew she lacked the raw speed of some of the others in the eight-woman lead pack. Leading slightly over the previous few laps, she had kept the pace strong so that her competitors couldn't catch their breath before the sprinting started. Now that there was only one lap to go, Huddle applied more pressure by surging into the first turn. Having to match Huddle's move would take some of the sting out of her rivals' kick in the final meters.

Her gambit appeared to work. The pack started to splinter. Gelete Burka of Ethiopia and Vivian Cheruiyot of Kenya passed Huddle on the backstretch, but Huddle was in third, the bronze-medal position, with half a lap to go. Huddle tried to latch on to Burka and Cheruiyot as they accelerated. Although she knew she probably couldn't keep pace with them, she might get pulled along far enough to discourage the women behind her.

Entering the final straightaway, Burka and Cheruiyot moved away from Huddle; Cheruiyot then easily dispatched

Burka for the win. Huddle kept charging, running on the line between the first and second lanes. One step before the finish line, she raised her arms to celebrate winning the bronze.

But she hadn't won the bronze. Her fellow American, Emily Infeld, had stuck close to Huddle over the last half lap. She clung to the inside of the first lane in the space afforded by Huddle running slightly wide. Head down, upper body bent, Infeld improbably closed on Huddle in the last 20 meters. When Huddle eased up ever so slightly to raise her arms, Infeld thrust her shoulders forward and nipped Huddle at the finish line. Infeld wound up beating Huddle—and winning the bronze medal—by nine hundredths of a second.

We tell this story about Huddle, who is an Olympian and American record holder, to show that even the best can falter. Her premature celebration is an extreme version of a common phenomenon. Many of us ease up in the final stretch of challenging situations. Although the consequences aren't usually as dramatic (and globally broadcast) as in Huddle's case, we still don't accomplish what we're capable of when we give less than our best effort to the very end.

FINISHING ON "E"

There are, of course, several reasons why we might not, literally or figuratively, run through the finish line. Like Molly Huddle at the 2015 world championships, we might have a momentary lapse in concentration. Many times it's for the simple reason that pushing ourselves to our limits hurts! In acute endeavors like a race or difficult workout, it's not a sign of weakness to think, "Sure would be nice to back off." As with most of the obstacles to success we've looked at in this book, the solution is to have the right countering strategies on hand.

For illustration, let's return one last time to Meb Keflezighi's victory at the 2014 Boston Marathon. If you watch the final 600 meters of the race, as Keflezighi makes his way down Boylston Street to the finish, you might think he'd had a relatively easy time of it. You'll see two runners not far off the lead, but Keflezighi doesn't look concerned. He repeatedly pumps both fists to acknowledge the crowd, he crosses himself at each of the two spots where bombs detonated during the previous year's marathon, and he even has the presence of mind in the final seconds to move his sunglasses to his forehead to improve the finish photos.

Those celebrations belie how horrible Keflezighi felt for the final few miles of the race. At mile 23, Keflezighi, who had been in the lead since mile 8, looked back. For the first time in more than an hour, he saw a competitor. Keflezighi knew the simple math—that runner must have been going much faster than him the last several miles. Keflezighi also knew that in such situations, it's often better to be the hunter than the hunted. The runner behind him, Wilson Chebet of Kenya, could see Keflezighi getting closer with each step. It's rare for someone who has been in the lead for a long time to be able to match the pace of someone catching up in the last part of a race.

At mile 24, Keflezighi thought about letting Chebet catch him. He told himself doing so would allow him to recover enough that he could then surge past Chebet in the final stretch on Boylston. Keflezighi acknowledged the thought, and quickly dismissed it as a by-product of his extreme fatigue. He told himself to take the opposite approach—to try to extend his gap on Chebet to dishearten his chaser.

He told himself this despite, as he wrote in his book *26 Marathons*, being at his physical and mental limits. A chronically tender spot on the ball of his left foot hurt every time that foot hit the ground. A hamstring strain he'd picked up a few weeks before Boston was on fire. Because he was pushing so hard to keep Chebet away, his stomach started bothering him, and he needed to vomit. Keflezighi didn't want Chebet to see him do so, lest Chebet know how badly Keflezighi was hurting, so he tilted his head back and swallowed his vomit.

Still Chebet closed. With about a mile to go, Keflezighi's lead was down to 6 seconds. He felt his running form deteriorate just when he most needed to run efficiently. He told himself, "Focus, focus, focus. Technique, technique, technique."

Another look back told Keflezighi that, although he hadn't extended his lead, Chebet was no longer cutting into it. Briefly concentrating on his running form had taken his mind off his fatigue while helping him to pick up the pace. He knew that if Chebet could have caught him, he would have by now; there would be no point in cat-and-mouse games at this stage of the race.

That realization brought Keflezighi a huge psychological boost. He rode that boost to the turn on Boylston Street, buoyed by the cheering crowd and thoughts of the previous year's bombing victims. The scenario he had visualized repeatedly in training—running the final stretch of the Boston Marathon en route to a win and a personal best— was about to come true.

HOW TO KEEP PRESSING

In the previous chapter we highlighted the key causes of failing to bring goal striving to a successful close. These were quitting too soon on a goal that's still achievable and continuing the futile chase of an unachievable goal.

But the story of Molly Huddle during the 2015 world championships highlights a final important issue in this regard: Sometimes we fail to achieve our goal because we withdraw our effort too quickly. This isn't the same as quitting too soon. Instead, as Huddle did in the final steps of that 10,000-meter race, sometimes when we feel we're on course to achieve our goal, and fully expect to be successful, we reduce our efforts, take our foot off the gas, and attempt to coast home.[1] And sometimes this means we just fall short!

There are a number of reasons for this. First, believing we're about to achieve a personally meaningful and important goal brings positive feelings. It's easy to imagine the elation Huddle might have felt as she approached that finish line, fully convinced that she was about to secure her ambition of a world championship medal. But as we learned in chapter 2, just as unpleasant emotions can sometimes be helpful, pleasant emotions can sometimes be unhelpful.

In terms of goal striving, it can be useful to think of our feelings and our actions as an input/output loop.[2] If we know we're behind on an important goal (input), we might feel concerned. We might respond by pushing harder on that goal (output). If the goal is achievable, then our concern was the trigger to change our focus and increase our efforts. Meb Keflezighi's thoughts over the final miles of the 2014 Boston Marathon demonstrate how concern that he might be caught helped to increase his focus and determination to cross the finish line first.

But the reverse is also true. If we know that we're making good progress toward achieving a meaningful goal (input), we tend to feel good. We might feel satisfaction or elation, depending on the magnitude of our goal. But these pleasant feelings can mean we shift our focus or reduce our efforts (output). This is especially true the closer we are to reaching our goal, and as we approach the finish line, we might, as Molly Huddle did, ease back too soon and attempt to coast home. In effect, our good feelings carry with them the message "I've done it! I don't need to work so hard anymore." And sometimes this means we just fall short.

A second reason we might lower our efforts on a goal we're progressing well on and close to achieving is overextension. Most of us have multiple goals in our lives that compete for our attention and efforts. When Noel was doing his final work on this book, he put less time and effort into other important areas of his life, such as his family and training to improve his fitness. It simply wouldn't have been possible to focus maximally on each one at the same time. He would have quickly become overextended and more likely to fail in each area.

Feeling good, or bad, about our progress allows us to prioritize different goals at different times. These feelings come with an important message—either we're doing well or we're falling behind. Doing well in one area can allow us to coast a little on that goal while putting time and effort into another area that might need attention. In doing so, we're able to invest in multiple goals without stretching our resources too thinly at any one time. Of course, sometimes we get caught in an overcommitment trap. We can decide which areas need our most urgent attention by using the decisional balance tool we introduced in chapter 11 ("When to Hold, When to Fold").

A study by researchers from Tilburg University in the Netherlands highlights how our progress, and subsequent feelings, shapes our focus and effort on different goals.[3] The researchers had eighty-two undergraduate students set a weight-loss goal over a three-week period. While this remained the primary goal, participants also identified a secondary goal they would like to achieve over the same time frame. The alternative goals included saving money, studying more, and spending time to help others. The researchers conducted the study in January to capture the typical New Year's resolutions that many of us set, yet struggle to see through to completion.

Over the three weeks, the students answered daily questions about their weight-loss goal and behaviors consistent with this goal, such as their food intake and their physical activity levels. They also rated the amount of effort they exerted in pursuing both their weight-loss goal and their secondary goal, how positive or negative they felt about their efforts, and how much progress they felt they were making toward achieving their goals.

The findings revealed that when participants felt that they were still far from achieving their weight-loss goal, yet were making good progress, positive feelings *increased* the effort they exerted to pursue their weight-loss goal and decreased the effort they exerted in pursuit of their secondary goal. In other words, early in the goal-striving process they prioritized their primary goal when they felt they were well on their way toward achieving it.

But when the students felt they were getting close to achieving their weight-loss goal, positive feelings prompted them to *decrease* their weight-loss efforts and increase the efforts they expended on their secondary goal. In this case, they prioritized efforts dedicated toward study time or actions to help others ahead of tasks, like physical activity, that were important for their almost-there-anyway weight-loss goals.

Despite the benefits of being able to prioritize different goals at different times, being aware that we can sometimes fall into the coasting trap can help us avoid situations like Molly Huddle's, where we just fall short on achieving important life goals. Fortunately, there are mental tools that can help.

In chapter 1, we learned about the difference between outcome goals, performance goals, and process goals. The goal to win a world championship medal, and the goal to achieve a weight-loss target, are examples of outcome goals. They're the result of the actions—or processes—we take to achieve them. Also in chapter 1, we highlighted some of the risks of focusing excessively on these goals ("Not All Goals Are Created Equal"). Foremost was the fact that thinking too much about the end result can mean we lose sight of the steps we need to take to get over the line in the first place.

Focusing on process goals, however, or the actions required to achieve an outcome, can help us avoid this pitfall. By doing so, we remain focused, one step at a time. As we learned in chapter 3 ("focus on control" tool), factors that we can control, or at least influence by using the mental techniques at our disposal, include how much effort we exert, our concentration, and our mental state. This idea is expressed by Meb Keflezighi's instructional mantra "Focus, focus, focus. Technique, technique, technique" ("self-talk" tool, chapter 4). Repeating that phrase helped him to remain focused and tune in to the important actions required to run as fast as possible over the final mile of the 2014 Boston Marathon ("The Case for Tuning In," chapter 3). Setting shorter-term sub-goals ("chunk it" tool, chapter 1) can also help you to stay focused, maintain your effort, and avoid coasting as you near the finish of your goal. As the end approaches, you might imagine telling yourself, "Just one more mile," or "Only another ten strides." For long-term projects, you might remind yourself, "All you have to do is bear down for the rest of the week, and then you'll be done."

As a final, controllable strategy, planning how you might respond if you're making good progress on your goals can be useful ("if you can keep your head" tool, chapter 1). This might seem counterintuitive. After all, if you're making good progress on a goal, why should you have a plan in place to deal with that? But as we've highlighted in this chapter, feeling good about our progress can come with unintended negative consequences. Using the if-then planning tool, you can plan to use any of the psychological techniques we identified in the previous paragraphs—depending on which ones you think best fit your needs—if you find you're coasting and in danger of missing out on your goal.

Planning to stay focused on the process and to maintain your effort levels, even if you're feeling good about your goal progress, can be an important step in successfully seeing your goals through to completion. By recognizing your triggers to coasting—such as your feelings or what you say to yourself—and responding in a productive way, you can make sustained focus and effort a positive habit to see you over the finish line ("make it a habit" tool, chapter 1).

ONE FINISH LINE LEADS TO THE NEXT START LINE

After you achieve a goal or complete a project, the first thing to do is celebrate. Take time to congratulate yourself on your accomplishment, thank and be grateful for the people who helped you reach it, and indulge in areas of pleasure you might have had to set aside while focusing on your just-completed goal. Spend time on other important areas of your life, like self-care, family, and friends, that you may have neglected during your goal-striving efforts.

Once the emotions of the moment have faded, perhaps two or three days later, it's time to once again draw on the genius of athletes. Do like winning teams do after a championship, and use the experience you just went through to set yourself up for more success in the future.

This is an important process to build your belief in what you're capable of achieving in future tasks ("previous accomplishments" tool, chapter 5). Do this in part by returning to the strengths profile we first mentioned way back in the introduction, and which you can find immediately after this chapter in appendix 1. Insert the same key mental qualities you identified the first time around, and rate your current ability on each of these qualities.

What we hope you'll notice is that your rating increased for each compared to the first time. Ideally, these new ratings are closer to the target ratings you initially set yourself.

Remember this key lesson: Your newly strengthened thinking skills are transferable. You can now apply them to a similar goal, or to something else entirely. These qualities are now an integral part of you. Whatever you focus on next, those tools will be there for you.

We also hope that you've learned the most valuable point this book makes. By learning how to think like an athlete, you now know that the mental qualities we've examined are malleable. None of them are set in stone. You can nurture and grow qualities like motivation, emotion regulation, concentration, resilience, and self-confidence. Although some are easier to cultivate than others, by learning and applying the right mental tools, you can improve each of these qualities. This continual process will help you succeed in the most important project of all—living a satisfying life.

My Strengths Profile

Strengths profiling is one tool that sport psychologists use with athletes during the early stages of a consultancy.[1] It's an invaluable self-discovery exercise that helps athletes reflect on the qualities needed to achieve success in their sport.[2]

Noel uses the technique both with athletes and with the students he teaches. For athletes, he asks them to reflect not only on psychological qualities but also on important aspects of their physical fitness, technical skills, tactical awareness, and lifestyle behaviors (e.g., sleep and nutrition). Reflecting on these qualities can help athletes raise their self-awareness, decide which qualities they need to work on, and set goals and targets for improvement.[3]

With students, Noel adapts the technique, asking them to complete a profile relevant to some aspect of their studies. So, an exam might be the performance setting, and like athletes reflecting on the qualities needed to perform successfully in their sport, Noel's students complete a profile on the qualities needed to perform successfully in their exams. For anyone, this can be a fun exercise to develop greater awareness of personal strengths and areas to target for improvement.

There are many variations of the profiling tool. In this appendix we've set out four key steps that are central to every version of the technique.[4]

STEP 1: IDENTIFY KEY MENTAL QUALITIES

To develop a strengths profile with athletes, Noel begins with a reflection on the key qualities required to be successful in their sport. Noel then asks them to write a list of these qualities, aiming to identify about twenty items. This is your starting point—a list of mental qualities important to you. When athletes produce their list, they typically include four or five psychological qualities alongside aspects of physical fitness, technical and tactical skills, and lifestyle behaviors. Don't worry if your list of mental qualities is much shorter than twenty items. Just write them in a column along the left-hand side of a page, leaving space for additional columns.

For athletes, the complete list will include mental qualities and also aspects of physical fitness, tactical awareness, and technical skills. So don't worry if your list of mental qualities is much shorter than twenty items.

This isn't a process to rush through. With athletes, Noel typically allots twenty to thirty minutes to reflect and generate as many qualities as they can think of during this first step.

To help generate the key qualities, Noel prompts athletes to reflect on the attributes of the highest-performing individual in their sport. He might also ask the athletes to think back to a competition when they performed at their best. He asks questions such as: Which qualities did you demonstrate when performing at your best? What were you thinking about at the time? How did you feel?

At this point, don't worry too much about the words you use to name each quality or attribute. As long as you know what it means, and it's relevant to you, that's what matters.

We've listed five qualities in the table below to help you get started. These are some of the most important psychological attributes for success among Olympic athletes.[5] But these qualities, among them being able to manage our emotions, relax when needed, and feel self-confident, are important for everyday life too.

Quality	My Current Rating	My Target Rating	How I Will Work on This
Motivation			
Ability to Stay Relaxed			
Concentration			
Emotion Management			
Self-Confidence			

STEP 2: YOUR CURRENT RATING

After you identify the key qualities important for you, the next step is to rate your current level on each of these qualities from 1 (very poor) to 10 (the best you could possibly be). This is your current rating.

Rating each of the qualities will help you to identify your strengths (higher scores) and areas that might need some development (lower scores). Writing these scores down is important; it can also help to record them in a column chart. Doing so will help you to visualize your strengths and more easily identify areas that you can improve on.

Below, we've added a current rating for each mental quality in our example. In this profile, you'll see that some qualities, such as motivation and concentration, are rated as strengths.

Quality	My Current Rating	My Target Rating	How I Will Work on This
Motivation	9		
Ability to Stay Relaxed	2		
Concentration	8		
Emotion Management	6		
Self-Confidence	4		

Becoming more aware of your strengths and weaknesses is important. Recognizing your character strengths can have an important impact on your mental health, improving how you feel and increasing your sense of life satisfaction.[6] In addition, knowing your strengths means you're more likely to use them in various life situations, thus making progress toward your goals.

STEP 3: YOUR TARGET RATING

Just as beneficial as recognizing your strengths is realizing what you need to work on and setting targets to improve in each of these areas. This is the third step in a strengths profile. In this step, you develop a second rating from 1 to 10 to indicate a score you would like to get to on each of your attributes. This is your target rating. We've completed this for our example in the table below.

Quality	My Current Rating	My Target Rating	How I Will Work on This
Motivation	9	9	
Ability to Stay Relaxed	2	4	
Concentration	8	8	
Emotion Management	6	6	
Self-Confidence	4	7	

Of course, we would all like to reach a 10 out of 10 on everything, but that isn't always realistic. Instead, athletes will focus on improving some of their weaker qualities. You can identify those that need the most work by calculating the difference between your current rating and your target rating. In our example, the difference score for staying relaxed is two points, whereas the difference score for self-confidence is three points.

You might also want to consider how important each of these qualities is to your overall performance. So, for example, although the ability to stay relaxed has the lowest current rating in the sample table, this individual might reflect that building self-confidence will be more important and may be the best quality to focus on first.

Once you have identified areas to work on, it's usually best to set a time frame for making these improvements. Let's say that building self-confidence is something you want to work on over the next month. In this short time frame, you might aim to improve this attribute by a little bit, perhaps by 2 to 3 points on the 1-to-10 scale. In a short time, this type of improvement is what's realistically achievable.

STEP 4: TAKING ACTION: HOW WILL YOU WORK ON THIS?

The final step is to consider how you'll work on each quality you've targeted. For our example, we might set goals for actions we can take to build self-confidence or to get better at being able to relax when we need to. We've included some suggestions in the table below.

Quality	My Current Rating	My Target Rating	How I Will Work on This
Motivation	9	9	
Ability to Stay Relaxed	2	4	Learn and practice one exercise that will help me to relax
Concentration	8	8	
Emotion Management	6	6	
Self-Confidence	4	7	Learn and use one tool to build my self-confidence

This is where the mental strategies and techniques presented throughout this book become useful. Chapter 1 will help you set appropriate goals and learn psychological strategies and techniques to achieve them. Tools to manage your emotions—like being able to relax when needed—are presented in chapter 2. Similarly, techniques you can use to build a more stable and robust level of self-confidence are presented in chapter 5.

A Sample Progressive Muscular Relaxation Script

(An audio recording of this script is available at youtu.be/EUEutXgfLXw.)

Progressive muscle relaxation is an exercise that reduces stress and anxiety in your body by having you slowly tense and then relax each muscle. While this exercise can provide an immediate feeling of relaxation, it's best to practice frequently, for about twenty minutes each time. With experience, you'll become more aware of when you experience tension, and you'll have the skills to help you relax when you do so.

During this exercise, each muscle should be tensed, but not to the point of strain. If you have any injuries or pain, you can skip the affected areas. Pay special attention to the feeling of releasing tension in each muscle and the resulting feeling of relaxation.

Let's begin.

Sit back or lie down in a comfortable position. Shut your eyes if you're comfortable doing so. Begin by taking a deep breath and noticing the feeling of air filling your lungs. Hold your breath for a few seconds.

(*Five-second pause*)

Release the breath slowly and let the tension leave your body.

Again, take another deep breath and hold it.

(*Five-second pause*)

Again, slowly release the air. Even slower now, take another breath. Fill your lungs and hold the air.

(*Five-second pause*)

Slowly release the breath and imagine the feeling of tension leaving your body.

Now, move your attention to your hands. With both hands together, make a tight fist, squeeze it as tight as you can, and relax, breathing out.

(*Five-second pause*)

Again, with both hands, make a tight fist, feel the tension in your hands and upper body, and relax, breathing out.

(*Five-second pause*)

Now move up to your upper arms, bend your elbows, and feel the tension in your upper arms.

(*Five-second pause*)

And relax, releasing and resting your hands back down.

Again, repeat the movement, bend your elbows, and take a deep breath. Feel the tension . . .

(*Five-second pause*)

And relax your hands back down, breathing out as you do so.

(*Five-second pause*)

Finally, stretch your arms out in front of you, feel the tension in the back of your upper arms. Breathe in and hold your breath . . .

(*Five-second pause*)

And relax, breathing back out.

As you breath slowly for a minute or so, notice the relaxation in your hands and upper arms. Slowly repeat to yourself, "I feel calm, I feel relaxed, I feel heavy and warm."

(*Sixty-second pause*)

Now we are going to move to your shoulders. Again, as you breathe in, shrug your shoulders up toward your ears. Hold this for a few seconds . . .

(*Five-second pause*)

And relax, breathing back out. As you do this, notice the difference between tension and relaxation in your shoulders. Repeat one more time.

(*Five-second pause*)

Again, take a few more deep breaths, and notice the feelings of relaxation in your hands, your arms, and your shoulders and upper back.

(*Sixty-second pause*)

Now we are going to move to your face. Starting with your eyes, squeeze them tightly shut, and feel the tension in your face, and around your eyes.

(*Five-second pause*)

And relax, breathing back out. Repeat this one more time.

(*Five-second pause*)

And relax, breathing back out again. Now moving to your forehead. Raise your eyebrows and take a deep breath, feeling the tension in your forehead.

(*Five-second pause*)

And relax, breathing back out. As you relax, notice your breathing become calm and relaxed.

(*Five-second pause*)

Now squeeze your jaw tightly shut. Clench your teeth and feel the tension in your jaw as you breathe in.

(*Five-second pause*)

And relax, letting your jaw relax as you breathe out.

Now we will move down to your lower back. Again, taking a deep breath, arch your back and feel the tension.

(*Five-second pause*)

And relax, breathing slowly back out. Repeat this one more time, and feel the tension, before slowly breathing back out and relaxing your back.

Now, for the next minute, take some slow, deep breaths. Each time you breathe out, notice the feelings of relaxation in your back, your shoulders, your face, down your arms, and all the way to your fingers. Slowly repeat to yourself, "I feel calm, I feel relaxed, I feel heavy and warm." Notice the feelings of relaxation spread throughout your body.

(*Sixty-second pause*)

Now we will focus just on your breathing. As you take a deep breath, and really notice the tension in your belly as you fill your lungs completely.

(*Five-second pause*)

And relax, breathing back out again. Repeat one more time.

(*Five-second pause*)

Now we will move to your lower body. Straighten your knees as much as you can and feel the tension in your thighs as you breathe in.

(*Five-second pause*)

And relax, breathing out. Repeat one more time, straightening both knees together and feeling the tension in your thighs as you breathe in.

(*Five-second pause*)

And relax, breathing back out.

Now move to the back of your legs. If you are sitting down, push your heels into the floor below you. If you are lying down, focus on stretching your heels away from your body. Again, breathe in as you feel the tension.

(*Five-second pause*)

And relax, breathing back out. Repeat one more time, feeling the tension in your legs.

(*Five-second pause*)

And relax, breathing out.

(*Five-second pause*)

And finally, focus on pulling your toes up toward your shins. Feel the tension in your lower leg as you breathe in.

(*Five-second pause*)

And relax, breathing out.

Next, focus on pointing your toes away from your body. Again, breathe in as you feel the tension.

(*Five-second pause*)

And relax, breathing out.

Finally, focus on curling your toes so you feel tension in the bottom of your foot. Again, breathe in as you do so and feel the tension.

(*Five-second pause*)

And relax, breathing out. Repeat one final time.

(*Five-second pause*)

And relax, breathing back out.

For the final few minutes, take a few more deep breaths. Each time you breathe in and out, notice the feelings of relaxation throughout your body: your face, your shoulders, your arms and hands, your back, and down your legs all the way to your toes. Just continue for a few minutes to enjoy that feeling of relaxation.

(*Longer pause*)

Finally, whenever you feel ready, stretch your arms and legs one last time and slowly open your eyes again.

Notes

_____

INTRODUCTION

1. Christiane Trottier and Sophie Robitaille, "Fostering Life Skills Development in High School and Community Sport: A Comparative Analysis of the Coach's Role," *Sport Psychologist* 28, no. 1 (March 2014): 10–21.

2. Nicholas L. Holt et al., "A Grounded Theory of Positive Youth Development Through Sport Based on Results from a Qualitative Meta-Study," *International Review of Sport and Exercise Psychology* 10, no.1 (January 2017): 1–49.

3. Aleksandar E. Chinkov and Nicholas L. Holt, "Implicit Transfer of Life Skills Through Participation in Brazilian Jiu-Jitsu," *Journal of Applied Sport Psychology* 28, no. 2 (2016): 139–53.

4. Girls on the Run, accessed January 6, 2021, girlsontherun.org.

5. Maureen R. Weiss et al., "Evaluating Girls on the Run in Promoting Positive Youth Development: Group Comparisons on Life Skills Transfer and Social Processes," *Pediatric Exercise Science* 32, no. 3 (July 2020): 1–11.

6. Maureen R. Weiss et al., "Girls on the Run: Impact of a Physical Activity Youth Development Program on Psychosocial and Behavioral Outcomes," *Pediatric Exercise Science* 31, no. 3 (August 2019): 330–40.

7. Ahead of the Game, accessed January 6, 2021, aheadofthegame.org.au.

8. Stewart A. Vella et al., "Ahead of the Game Protocol: A Multi-Component, Community Sport-Based Program Targeting Prevention, Promotion and Early Intervention for Mental Health Among Adolescent Males," *BMC Public Health* 18, no. 1 (March 2018): 390.

9. Stewart A. Vella et al., "An Intervention for Mental Health Literacy and Resilience in Organized Sports," *Medicine and Science in Sports and Exercise* 53, no. 1 (January 2021): 139–49.

10. "Projects," The SPRINT Project, accessed January 6, 2021, sprintproject.org/projects.

11. Benjamin Parry, Mary Quinton, and Jennifer Cumming, *Mental Skills Training Toolkit: A Resource for Strengths-Based Development* (Birmingham, UK: University of Birmingham, 2020), stbasils.org.uk/wp-content/uploads/2020/01/MST-toolkit-final.pdf.

12. Sam J. Cooley et al., "The Experiences of Homeless Youth When Using Strengths Profiling to Identify Their Character Strengths," *Frontiers in Psychology* 10 (2019): 2036.

CHAPTER 1

1. Bernd Heinrich, *Why We Run: A Natural History* (New York: HarperCollins, 2001), 177.

2. Kieran M. Kingston and Lew Hardy, "Effects of Different Types of Goals on Processes That Support Performance," *Sport Psychologist* 11, no. 3 (September 1997): 277–93.

3. Gerard H Seijts, Gary P. Latham, and Meredith Woodwark, "Learning Goals: A Qualitative and Quantitative Review," in *New Developments in Goal Setting and Task Performance*, ed. Edwin A. Locke and Gary P. Latham (New York: Routledge, 2013), 195–12.

4. "Interview with Rory McIlroy - Setting Goals and Maintaining Motivation," Santander UK, video, 5:27, February 7, 2014, youtube.com/watch?v=breTsCJbui8.

5. Noel Brick, Tadhg MacIntyre, and Mark Campbell, "Metacognitive Processes in the Self-Regulation of Performance in Elite Endurance Runners," *Psychology of Sport and Exercise* 19 (July 2015): 1–9.

6. L. Blaine Kyllo and Daniel M. Landers, "Goal Setting in Sport and Exercise: A Research Synthesis to Resolve the Controversy," *Journal of Sport and Exercise Psychology* 17, no. 2 (1995): 117–37.

7. Jennifer Stock and Daniel Cervone, "Proximal Goal-Setting and Self-Regulatory Processes," *Cognitive Therapy and Research* 14, no. 5 (October 1990): 483–98.

8. Ayelet Fishbach, Ravi Dhar, and Ying Zhang, "Subgoals as Substitutes or Complements: The Role of Goal Accessibility," *Journal of Personality and Social Psychology* 91, no. 2 (September 2006): 232–42.

9. "Player Numbers," World Rugby, January 1, 2017, accessed June 1, 2020, world.rugby/development/player-numbers?lang=en.

10. Richie McCaw, *The Real McCaw: The Autobiography* (London: Aurum Press, 2012), 13.

11. Greg Stutchbury, "G.A.B. McCaw Goes Out on Top of the Heap," Reuters, November 18, 2015, reuters.com/article/uk-rugby-union-mccaw-newsmaker/g-a-b-mccaw-goes-out-on-top-of-the-heap-idUKKCN0T805H20151119.

12. Robert Weinberg et al., "Perceived Goal Setting Practices of Olympic Athletes: An Exploratory Investigation," *Sport Psychologist* 14, no. 3 (September 2000): 279–95.

13. Laura Healy, Alison Tincknell-Smith, and Nikos Ntoumanis, "Goal Setting in Sport and Performance," in *Oxford Research Encyclopedia of Psychology* (Oxford: Oxford University Press, 2018), 1–23.

14. Christian Swann et al., "Comparing the Effects of Goal Types in a Walking Session with Healthy Adults: Preliminary Evidence for Open Goals in Physical Activity," *Psychology of Sport and Exercise* 47 (March 2020): 1–10.

15. Rebecca M. Hawkins et al., "The Effects of Goal Types on Psychological Outcomes in Active and Insufficiently Active Adults in a Walking Task: Further Evidence for Open Goals," *Psychology of Sport and Exercise* 48 (May 2020): 101661.

16. Paschal Sheeran and Thomas L. Webb, "The Intention–Behavior Gap," *Social and Personality Psychology Compass* 10, no. 9 (September 2016): 503–18.

17. Peter M. Gollwitzer, "Implementation Intentions: Strong Effects of Simple Plans," *American Psychologist* 54, no. 7 (July 1999): 493–503.

18. Patrick Mahomes, "NFL Draft Cover Letter," *Players' Tribune*, April 27, 2017, theplayerstribune.com/en-us/articles/patrick-mahomes-ii-texas-tech-nfl-draft-cover-letter.

19. Anja Achtziger, Peter M. Gollwitzer, and Paschal Sheeran, "Implementation Intentions and Shielding Goal Striving from Unwanted Thoughts and Feelings," *Personality and Social Psychology Bulletin* 34, no. 3 (March 2008): 381–93.

20. Bob Bowman with Charles Butler, *The Golden Rules: Finding World-Class Excellence in Your Life and Work* (London: Piatkus, 2016), 188.

21. Peter M. Gollwitzer and Paschal Sheeran, "Implementation Intentions and Goal Achievement: A Meta-Analysis of Effects and Processes," *Advances in Experimental Social Psychology* 38, no. 6 (December 2006): 69–119.

22. Charles Duhigg, *The Power of Habit: Why We Do What We Do in Life and Business* (New York: Random House, 2012), 114.

23. Phillippa Lally and Benjamin Gardner, "Promoting Habit Formation," *Health Psychology Review* 7, supplement 1 (May 2013): S137-S158.

24. Benjamin Gardner, Phillippa Lally, and Amanda L. Rebar, "Does Habit Weaken the Relationship Between Intention and Behaviour? Revisiting the Habit-Intention Interaction Hypothesis," *Social and Personality Psychology Compass* 14, no. 8 (August 2020): e12553.

25. David T. Neal et al., "How Do Habits Guide Behavior? Perceived and Actual Triggers of Habits in Daily Life," *Journal of Experimental Social Psychology* 48, no. 2 (March 2012): 492–98.

26. Jeffrey M. Quinn et al., "Can't Control Yourself? Monitor Those Bad Habits," *Personality and Social Psychology Bulletin* 36, no. 4 (April 2010): 499–511.

27. Phillippa Lally et al., "How Are Habits Formed: Modelling Habit Formation in the Real World," *European Journal of Social Psychology* 40, no. 6 (October 2010): 998–1009.

CHAPTER 2

1. All Blacks Match Centre, accessed June 1, 2020, stats. allblacks.com.

2. Chris Rattue, "France Pose Absolutely No Threat to the All Blacks," *New Zealand Herald*, October 2, 2007, nzherald. co.nz/sport/ichris-rattuei-france-pose-absolutely-no-threat-to-the-all-blacks. CVUXP4NLMHI6DINQRKFVHMUH6U.

3. Christopher Mesagno and Denise M. Hill, "Definition of Choking in Sport: Re-conceptualization and Debate," *International Journal of Sport Psychology* 44, no. 4 (July 2013): 267–77.

4. Ceri Evans, *Perform Under Pressure: Change the Way You Feel, Think and Act Under Pressure* (London: Thorsons, 2019).

5. Julie K. Norem and Edward C. Chang, "The Positive Psychology of Negative Thinking," *Journal of Clinical Psychology* 58, no. 9 (September 2002): 993–101.

6. James A. Russell, "A Circumplex Model of Affect," *Journal of Personality and Social Psychology* 39, no. 6 (December 1980): 1161–78.

7. Jonathan Posner, James A. Russell, and Bradley S. Peterson, "The Circumplex Model of Affect: An Integrative Approach to Affective Neuroscience, Cognitive Development, and Psychopathology," *Development and Psychopathology* 17, no. 3 (Summer 2005): 715–34.

8. Scott Douglas, *Running Is My Therapy: Relieve Stress and Anxiety, Fight Depression, Ditch Bad Habits, and Live Happier* (New York: The Experiment, 2018).

9. Jared B. Torre and Matthew D. Lieberman, "Putting Feelings into Words: Affect Labeling as Implicit Emotion Regulation," *Emotion Review* 10, no. 2 (March 2018): 116–24.

10. Brian Parkinson and Peter Totterdell, "Classifying Affect-Regulation Strategies," *Cognition and Emotion* 13, no. 3 (1999): 277–303.

11. Damian M. Stanley et al., "Emotion Regulation Strategies Used in the Hour Before Running," *International Journal of Sport and Exercise Psychology* 10, no. 3 (April 2012): 159–71.

12. Adam A. Augustine and Scott H. Hemenover, "On the Relative Effectiveness of Affect Regulation Strategies: A Meta-analysis," *Cognition and Emotion* 23, no. 6 (July 2009): 1181–220.

13. Christopher R. D. Wagstaff, "Emotion Regulation and Sport Performance," *Journal of Sport and Exercise Psychology* 36, no. 4 (August 2014): 401–12.

14. Dorota Kobylińska and Petko Kusev, "Flexible Emotion Regulation: How Situational Demands and Individual Differences Influence the Effectiveness of Regulatory Strategies," *Frontiers in Psychology* 10 (2019): 72.

15. Kevin N. Ochsner and James J. Gross, "Cognitive Emotion Regulation: Insights from Social Cognitive and Affective Neuroscience," *Current Directions in Psychological Science* 17, no. 2 (April 2008): 153–58.

16. Faye F. Didymus and David Fletcher, "Effects of a Cognitive-Behavioral Intervention on Field Hockey Players' Appraisals of Organizational Stressors," *Psychology of Sport and Exercise* 30 (May 2017): 173–85.

17. James J. Gross and Ross A. Thompson, "Emotion Regulation Conceptual Foundations," in *Handbook of Emotion Regulation*, ed. James J. Gross (New York: Guilford Press, 2007), 3–24.

18. Owen Thomas, Ian Maynard, and Sheldon Hanton, "Intervening with Athletes During the Time Leading Up to Competition: Theory to Practice II," *Journal of Applied Sport Psychology* 19, no. 4 (October 2007): 398–418.

19. Brian Costello, "How Stephen Gostkowski Handles His Super Bowl Nerves," *New York Post*, January 31, 2019, nypost.com/2019/01/31/how-stephen-gostkowski-handles-his-super-bowl-nerves/#.

20. Alison Wood Brooks, "Get Excited: Reappraising Pre-performance Anxiety as Excitement," *Journal of Experimental Psychology: General* 143 no. 3 (June 2014): 1144–58.

21. Philip M. Ullrich and Susan K. Lutgendorf, "Journaling About Stressful Events: Effects of Cognitive Processing and Emotional Expression," *Annals of Behavioral Medicine* 24, no. 3 (Summer 2002): 244–50.

22. Golnaz Tabibnia, "An Affective Neuroscience Model of Boosting Resilience in Adults," *Neuroscience and Biobehavioral Reviews* 115 (August 2020): 321–50.

23. Scott H. Hemenover, "The Good, the Bad, and the Healthy: Impacts of Emotional Disclosure of Trauma on Resilient Self-Concept and Psychological Distress," *Personality and Social Psychology Bulletin* 29, no. 10 (October 2003): 1236–44.

24. Venus Williams and Serena Williams with Hilary Beard, *Venus and Serena: Serving from the Hip* (Boston: Houghton Mifflin, 2005), 114.

25. Howard Fendrich, "'To Everybody, It's My 1st Olympics, but to Me, It's My 1,000th': Journals Help Shiffrin Prep," *U.S. News and World Report*, February 17, 2014, usnews.com/news/sports/articles/2014/02/17/us-teen-shiffrins-notes-helped-prep-for-olympics.

26. Paulo S. Boggio et al., "Writing About Gratitude Increases Emotion-Regulation Efficacy," *Journal of Positive Psychology* 15, no. 6 (August 2019): 783–94.

27. Kristine Thomason, "Olympic Sprinter Allyson Felix Shares Her Go-To Core Workout and How She Stays Motivated," *Mind Body Green*, November 26, 2020, mindbodygreen.com/articles/olympic-sprinter-allyson-felix-training-routine.

28. Helene Elliott, "She's Been Tested, and Allyson Felix Is Confident, 'Still Hungry' and 'Very Secure in Who I Am,'" *Los Angeles Times*, March 9, 2020, latimes.com/sports/story/2020-03-09/allyson-felix-track-field-olympics-usc.

29. Sarah Kate McGowan and Evelyn Behar, "A Preliminary Investigation of Stimulus Control Training for Worry: Effects on Anxiety and Insomnia," *Behavior Modification* 37, no. 1 (January 2013): 90–112.

30. Jen Nash, "Stress and Diabetes: The Use of 'Worry Time' as a Way of Managing Stress," *Journal of Diabetes Nursing* 18, no. 8 (2014): 329–33.

31. Karen Haddad and Patsy Tremayne, "The Effects of Centering on the Free-Throw Shooting Performance of Young Athletes," *Sport Psychologist* 23, no. 1 (March 2009): 118–36.

32. Lisa J. Rogerson and Dennis W. Hrycaiko, "Enhancing Competitive Performance of Ice Hockey Goaltenders Using Centering and Self-Talk," *Journal of Applied Sport Psychology* 14 no. 1 (March 2002): 14–26.

33. Maureen R. Weiss et al., "Evaluating Girls on the Run in Promoting Positive Youth Development: Group Comparisons on Life Skills Transfer and Social Processes," *Pediatric Exercise Science* 32, no. 3 (August 2020): 172–82.

34. Laura A. Pawlow and Gary E. Jones, "The Impact of Abbreviated Progressive Muscle Relaxation on Salivary Cortisol," *Biological Psychology* 60 no. 1 (July 2002): 1–16.

35. Martha S. McCallie, Claire M. Blum, and Charlaine J. Hood, "Progressive Muscle Relaxation," *Journal of Human Behavior in the Social Environment* 13, no. 3 (July 2006): 51–66.

36. Richie McCaw, *The Real McCaw: The Autobiography* (London: Aurum Press, 2012), 181–82.

CHAPTER 3

1. Noel Brick, Tadhg MacIntyre, and Mark Campbell, "Metacognitive Processes in the Self-Regulation of Performance in Elite Endurance Runners," *Psychology of Sport and Exercise* 19 (July 2015): 1–9.

2. William P. Morgan and Michael L. Pollock, "Psychologic Characterization of the Elite Distance Runner," *Annals of the New York Academy of Sciences* 301, no. 1 (October 1977): 382–403.

3. Noel Brick, Tadhg MacIntyre, and Mark Campbell, "Attentional Focus in Endurance Activity: New Paradigms and Future Directions," *International Review of Sport and Exercise Psychology* 7, no. 1 (February 2014): 106–34.

4. Noel Brick et al., "Metacognitive Processes and Attentional Focus in Recreational Endurance Runners," *International Journal of Sport and Exercise Psychology* 18, no. 3 (September 2020): 362–79.

5. Peter Aspinall et al., "The Urban Brain: Analysing Outdoor Physical Activity with Mobile EEG," *British Journal of Sports Medicine* 49, no. 4 (February 2015): 272–76.

6. Gregory N. Bratman et al., "Nature Reduces Rumination and Subgenual Prefrontal Cortex Activation," *Proceedings of the National Academy of Sciences* 112, no. 28 (July 2015): 8567–72.

7. Tadhg E. MacIntyre et al., "An Exploratory Study of Extreme Sport Athletes' Nature Interactions: From Well-Being to Pro-environmental Behavior," *Frontiers in Psychology* 10 (May 2019): 1233.

8. Rick A. LaCaille, Kevin S. Masters, and Edward M. Heath, "Effects of Cognitive Strategy and Exercise Setting on Running Performance, Perceived Exertion, Affect, and Satisfaction," *Psychology of Sport and Exercise* 5, no. 4 (October 2004): 461–76.

9. Charles M. Farmer, Keli A. Braitman, and Adrian K. Lund, "Cell Phone Use While Driving and Attributable Crash Risk," *Traffic Injury Prevention* 11, no. 5 (October 2010): 466–70.

10. Cédric Galéra et al., "Mind Wandering and Driving: Responsibility Case-Control Study," *British Medical Journal* 345, no. 7888 (December 2012): e8105.

11. David Kane, "'I'm on Cloud 9'—Andreescu Opens Up on Sky-High Confidence, Conquering Doubts with US Open Crown," *WTA Tour*, September 8, 2019, wtatennis.com/news/1445478/im-on-cloud-9-andreescu-opens-up-on-sky-high-confidence-conquering-doubts-with-us-open-crown.

12. Frank L. Gardner and Zella E. Moore, "A Mindfulness-Acceptance-Commitment-Based Approach to Athletic Performance Enhancement: Theoretical Considerations," *Behavior Therapy* 35, no. 4 (Autumn 2004): 707–23.

13. Emilie Thienot and Danielle Adams, "Mindfulness in Endurance Performance," in *Endurance Performance in Sport: Psychological Theory and Interventions*, ed. Carla Meijen (London: Routledge, 2019), 168–82.

14. Stephanie Livaudais, "'The First Thing I Do Is Meditate': Bianca Andreescu Visualizes Indian Wells Success," March 14, 2019, wtatennis.com/news/1449622/ -first-thing-i-do-meditate-bianca-andreescu- visualizes-indian-wells-success.

15. Lori Haase et al., "A Pilot Study Investigating Changes in Neural Processing After Mindfulness Training in Elite Athletes," *Frontiers in Behavioral Neuroscience* 9 (August 2015): 229.

16. Douglas C. Johnson et al., "Modifying Resilience Mechanisms in At-Risk Individuals: A Controlled Study of Mindfulness Training in Marines Preparing for Deployment," *American Journal of Psychiatry* 171, no. 8 (August 2014): 844–53.

17. Michael Noetel et al., "Mindfulness and Acceptance Approaches to Sporting Performance Enhancement: A Systematic Review," *International Review of Sport and Exercise Psychology* 12, no. 3 (November 2017): 1–37.

18. Stuart Cathcart, Matt McGregor, and Emma Groundwater, "Mindfulness and Flow in Elite Athletes," *Journal of Clinical Sport Psychology* 8, no. 2 (January 2014): 119–41.

19. Cian Ahearne, Aidan P. Moran, and Chris Lonsdale, "The Effect of Mindfulness Training on Athletes' Flow: An Initial Investigation," *Sport Psychologist* 25, no. 2 (June 2011): 177–89.

20. "Kobe Bryant Explains 'Being in the Zone,'" You Exist Externally Here, video, 2:38, August 19, 2013, youtube. com/watch?v=wl49zc8g3DY.

21. Mihaly Csikszentmihalyi, *Flow: The Psychology of Optimal Experience*, 2nd ed. (New York: Harper & Row, 2002), 72-93.

22. Jeanne Nakamura and Mihaly Csikszentmihalyi, "The Concept of Flow," in *Handbook of Positive Psychology*, ed. C. R. Snyder and Shane J. Lopez (New York: Oxford University Press, 2002), 89–105.

23. Christian Swann et al., "Psychological States Underlying Excellent Performance in Professional Golfers: 'Letting It Happen' vs. 'Making It Happen,'" *Psychology of Sport and Exercise* 23 (March 2016): 101–13.

24. Christian Swann et al., "Psychological States Underlying Excellent Performance in Sport: Toward an Integrated Model of Flow and Clutch States," *Journal of Applied Sport Psychology* 29, no. 4 (2017): 375–401.

25. Josephine Perry, *Performing Under Pressure: Psychological Strategies for Sporting Success* (London: Routledge, 2020), 135–37.

26. Martin Turner and Jamie Barker, *Tipping the Balance: The Mental Skills Handbook for Athletes* (Oakamoor, UK: Bennion Kearny, 2014), 101–40.

27. Marc V. Jones et al., "A Theory of Challenge and Threat States in Athletes," *International Review of Sport and Exercise Psychology* 2, no. 2 (2009): 161–80.

28. Aidan P. Moran, *The Psychology of Concentration in Sport Performers: A Cognitive Analysis* (East Sussex, UK: Psychology Press, 1996), 149.

29. Stewart Cotterill, "Pre-performance Routines in Sport: Current Understanding and Future Directions," *International Review of Sport and Exercise Psychology* 3, no. 2 (September 2010): 132–53.

30. Glasgow Caledonian University, "Elite Golfers Share Secrets of Success to Help Budding Sports Stars," March 24, 2020, gcu.ac.uk/theuniversity/universitynew s/2020-elitegolferssharesecretsofsuccess/.

31. Alex Oliver, Paul J. McCarthy, and Lindsey Burns, "A Grounded-Theory Study of Meta-attention in Golfers," *Sport Psychologist* 34, no. 1 (March 2020): 11–22.

32. Dave Alred, *The Pressure Principle: Handle Stress, Harness Energy, and Perform When It Counts* (London: Penguin Life, 2017), 66-67.

33. Jackie MacMullan, "Rise Above It or Drown: How Elite NBA Athletes Handle Pressure," ESPN, May 29, 2019, espn.co.uk/nba/story/_/id/26802987/rise-drown-how-elit e-nba-athletes-handle-pressure.

CHAPTER 4

1. Chloe Gray, "Dina Asher-Smith Just Gave Us an Amazing Lesson on How to Be Better Than Ever," accessed July 9, 2020, stylist.co.uk/people/dina-asher-smith-nike-interview-training-plan/350606.

2. Noel Brick et al., "Metacognitive Processes and Attentional Focus in Recreational Endurance Runners," *International Journal of Sport and Exercise Psychology* 18, no. 3 (September 2020): 362–79.

3. Kalina Christoff, Alan Gordon, and Rachelle Smith, "The Role of Spontaneous Thought in Human Cognition," in *Neuroscience of Decision Making*, ed. Oshin Vartanian and David R. Mandel (New York: Psychological Press, 2011), 259–84.

4. "Sports Players Use Self Talk," ThinkSRSD, video, 6:24, September 26, 2017, youtube.com/watch?v=-BKWlMBleYQ.

5. Anthony William Blanchfield et al., "Talking Yourself out of Exhaustion: The Effects of Self-Talk on Endurance Performance," *Medicine and Science in Sports and Exercise* 46, no. 5 (May 2014): 998–1007.

6. Julia Schüler and Thomas A. Langens, "Psychological Crisis in a Marathon and the Buffering Effects of Self-Verbalizations," *Journal of Applied Social Psychology* 37, no. 10 (October 2007): 2319–44.

7. Antonis Hatzigeorgiadis et al., "Self-Talk and Sport Performance: A Meta-analysis," *Perspectives on Psychological Science* 6, no. 4 (July 2011): 348–56.

8. David Tod, James Hardy, and Emily Oliver, "Effects of Self-Talk: A Systematic Review," *Journal of Sport and Exercise Psychology* 33, no. 5 (October 2011): 666–87.

9. Judy L. Van Raalte, Andrew Vincent, and Britton W. Brewer, "Self-Talk: Review and Sport-Specific Model," *Psychology of Sport and Exercise* 22 (January 2016): 139–48.

10. Christopher E. J. DeWolfe, David Scott, and Kenneth A. Seaman, "Embrace the Challenge: Acknowledging a Challenge Following Negative Self-Talk Improves Performance," *Journal of Applied Sport Psychology* (August 2020).

11. "Tommy Haas Talking to Himself," CarstenL01, video, 2:35, December 30, 2008, youtube.com/watch?v=8gQ2NhteF44.

12. James Hardy, Aled V. Thomas, and Anthony W. Blanchfield, "To Me, to You: How You Say Things Matters for Endurance Performance," *Journal of Sports Sciences* 37, no. 18 (September 2019): 2122–30.

13. Thomas L. Webb, Eleanor Miles, and Paschal Sheeran, "Dealing with Feeling: A Meta-analysis of the Effectiveness of Strategies Derived from the Process Model of Emotion Regulation," *Psychological Bulletin* 138, no. 4 (July 2012): 775–808.

14. E. Kross and O. Ayduk, "Self-Distancing: Theory, Research, and Current Directions," in *Advances in Experimental Social Psychology*, ed. James M. Olson, vol. 55 (New York: Elsevier, 2017), 81–136.

15. Ethan Kross et al., "Self-Talk as a Regulatory Mechanism: How You Do It Matters," *Journal of Personality and Social Psychology* 106, no. 2 (February 2014): 304–24.

16. Jon Greenberg, "Exiting via the Low Road," ESPN, July 9, 2010, espn.com/chicago/nba/columns/story?id=5365985.

17. Antonis Hatzigeorgiadis et al., "Self-Talk," in *Routledge Companion to Sport and Exercise Psychology: Global Perspectives and Fundamental Concepts*, ed. Athanasios G. Papaioannou and Dieter Hackfort (London: Taylor and Francis, 2014), 370–83.

18. Alister McCormick and Antonis Hatzigeorgiadis, "Self-Talk and Endurance Performance," in *Endurance Performance in Sport: Psychological Theory and Interventions*, ed. Carla Meijen (London: Routledge, 2019) 152–67.

19. Richard Bennett and Martin Turner, "The Theory and Practice of Rational Emotive Behavior Therapy (REBT)," in *Rational Emotive Behavior Therapy in Sport and Exercise*, ed. Martin Turner and Richard Bennett (London: Routledge, 2020), 4–19

CHAPTER 5

1. Robin S. Vealey, "Confidence in Sport," in *Handbook of Sports Medicine and Science: Sport Psychology*, ed. Britton W. Brewer (Oxford: Wiley-Blackwell, 2009), 43–52.

2. "'I'm Aware of the Streak, but It Means Nothing,' Says Novak Djokovic Ahead of Dubai Test," *Tennishead*, February 24, 2020, tennishead.net/im-aware-of-th e-streak-but-it-means-nothing-says-novak -djokovic-ahead-of-dubai-test/.

3. Albert Bandura, *Social Foundations of Thought and Action: A Social Cognitive Theory* (Englewood Cliffs, NJ: Prentice Hall, 1986).

4. Albert Bandura, "Self-Efficacy: Toward a Unifying Theory of Behavioral Change," *Psychological Review*, 84, no. 2 (March 1977): 191–215.

5. Deborah L. Feltz and Cathy D. Lirgg, "Self-Efficacy Beliefs of Athletes, Teams, and Coaches," in *Handbook of Sport Psychology*, 2nd ed., ed. Robert N. Singer, Heather A. Hausenblas, and Christopher M. Janelle (New York: John Wiley & Sons, 2001), 340–61.

6. Ellen L. Usher and Frank Pajares, "Sources of Self-Efficacy in School: Critical Review of the Literature and Future Directions," *Review of Educational Research* 78, no. 4 (December 2008): 751–96.

7. James E. Maddux, "Self-Efficacy Theory: An Introduction," in *Self-Efficacy, Adaptation, and Adjustment: Theory, Research, and Application*, ed. James E. Maddux (New York: Plenum, 1995), 3–33.

8. Simon Middlemas and Chris Harwood, "A Pre-Match Video Self-Modeling Intervention in Elite Youth Football," *Journal of Applied Sport Psychology* 32, no. 5 (2020): 450–75.

9. Robert S. Vealey et al., "Sources of Sport-Confidence: Conceptualization and Instrument Development," *Journal of Sport and Exercise Psychology* 21, no. 1 (1998): 54–80.

10. Kate Hays et al., "Sources and Types of Confidence Identified by World Class Sport Performers," *Journal of Applied Sport Psychology* 19, no. 4 (October 2007): 434–56.

11. Kieran Kingston, Andrew Lane, and Owen Thomas, "A Temporal Examination of Elite Performers Sources of Sport-Confidence," *Sport Psychologist* 24, no. 3 (2010): 313–32.

12. "Jack Nicklaus Quotes," BrainyQuote, accessed July 10, 2020, brainyquote.com/quotes/jack_nicklaus_159073.

13. Josephine Perry, *Performing Under Pressure: Psychological Strategies for Sporting Success* (London: Routledge, 2020), 179-180.

14. Krista Munroe-Chandler, Craig Hall, and Graham Fishburne, "Playing with Confidence: The Relationship Between Imagery Use and Self-Confidence and Self-Efficacy in Youth Soccer Players," *Journal of Sports Sciences* 26, no. 14 (December 2008): 1539–46.

15. Karen Price, "How Diver Katrina Young and Team USA Athletes Are Still Going In to Practice—Without Actually Going to Practice," *Team USA*, May 20, 2020, teamusa.org/News/2020/May/20/Diver-Katrina-Young-Team-USA-Athletes-Going-In-To-Practice-Without-Going-To-Practice.

16. Greg Bishop, "How Deontay Wilder Uses Meditation to Visualize His Fights Before They Happen," *Sports Illustrated*, November 21, 2019, si.com/boxing/2019/11/21/deonaty-wilder-luis-ortiz-meditation.

CHAPTER 6

1. Sharon R. Sears, Annette L. Stanton, and Sharon Danoff-Burg, "The Yellow Brick Road and the Emerald City: Benefit Finding, Positive Reappraisal Coping and Posttraumatic Growth in Women with Early-Stage Breast Cancer," *Health Psychology* 22, no. 5 (September 2003): 487–97.

2. Scott Cresswell and Ken Hodge, "Coping with Stress in Elite Sport: A Qualitative Analysis of Elite Surf Lifesaving Athletes," *New Zealand Journal of Sports Medicine* 29, no. 4 (Summer 2001): 78–83.

3. Anne-Josée Guimond, Hans Ivers, and Josée Savard, "Is Emotion Regulation Associated with Cancer-Related Psychological Symptoms," *Psychology & Health*, 24 no. 1 (January 2019): 44-63.

4. Sam J. Cooley et al., "The Experiences of Homeless Youth When Using Strengths Profiling to Identify Their Character Strengths," *Frontiers in Psychology* 10 (September 2019): 2036.

5. Sunghee Park, David Lavallee, and David Tod, "Athletes' Career Transition Out of Sport: A Systematic Review," *International Review of Sport and Exercise Psychology* 6, no. 1 (January 2012): 22–53.

6. Natalia Stambulova, "Counseling Athletes in Career Transitions: The Five-Step Career Planning Strategy," *Journal of Sport Psychology in Action* 1, no. 2 (November 2010): 95–105.

7. David Fletcher and Mustafa Sarkar, "Psychological Resilience: A Review and Critique of Definitions, Concepts, and Theory," *European Psychologist* 18, no. 1 (April 2013): 12–23.

8. David Fletcher and Mustafa Sarkar, "Mental Fortitude Training: An Evidence-Based Approach to Developing Psychological Resilience for Sustained Success," *Journal of Sport Psychology in Action* 7, no. 3 (December 2016): 135–57.

9. Christopher Bryan, Deirdre O'Shea, and Tadhg MacIntyre, "Stressing the Relevance of Resilience: A Systematic Review of Resilience Across the Domains of Sport and Work," *International Review of Sport and Exercise Psychology* 12, no. 1 (July 2019): 70–111.

10. David Fletcher and Mustafa Sarkar, "A Grounded Theory of Psychological Resilience in Olympic Champions," *Psychology of Sport and Exercise* 13, no. 5 (September 2012): 669–78.

11. Patrick Fletcher, "Peter Sagan: I Missed My Opportunity at World Championships," *Cycling News*, September 29, 2019, cyclingnews.com/news/peter-sagan-i-missed-my-opportunity-at-world-championships.

12. Jesse Harriott and Joseph R. Ferrari, "Prevalence of Procrastination Among Samples of Adults," *Psychological Reports* 78, no. 2 (April 1996): 611–16.

13. Jay L. Zagorsky, "Why Most of Us Procrastinate in Filing Our Taxes—and Why It Doesn't Make Any Sense," *Conversation*, April 13, 2015, theconversation.com/why-most-of-us-procrastinate-in-filing-our-

taxes-and-why-it-doesnt-make-any-sense-39766.

14. Thor Gamst-Klaussen, Piers Steel, and Frode Svartdal, "Procrastination and Personal Finances: Exploring the Roles of Planning and Financial Self-Efficacy," *Frontiers in Psychology* 10 (April 2019): 775.

15. Piers Steel, "The Nature of Procrastination: A Meta-analytic and Theoretical Review of Quintessential Self-Regulatory Failure," *Psychological Bulletin* 133, no. 1 (January 2007), 65–94.

16. Craig Pickering, "The Mundanity of Excellence," HMMR Media, September 4, 2020, http://hmmrmedia.com/2020/09/the-mundanity-of-excellence.

17. Daniel F. Chambliss, "The Mundanity of Excellence: An Ethnographic Report on Stratification and Olympic Swimmers," *Sociological Theory* 7, no. 1 (Spring 1989): 70–86.

CHAPTER 7

1. Graham D. Bodie, "A Racing Heart, Rattling Knees, and Ruminative Thoughts: Defining, Explaining, and Treating Public Speaking Anxiety," *Communication Education* 59, no. 1 (January 2010): 70–105.

2. Ewa Mörtberg et al., "Psychometric Properties of the Personal Report of Public Speaking Anxiety (PRPSA) in a Sample of University Students in Sweden," *International Journal of Cognitive Therapy* 11, no. 4 (December 2018), 421–33.

3. Marc Jones et al., "A Theory of Challenge and Threat States in Athletes," *International Review of Sport and Exercise Psychology* 2, no. 2 (September 2019): 161–80.

4. Andrew J. Elliot and Holly A. McGregor, "A 2 × 2 Achievement Goal Framework," *Journal of Personality and Social Psychology* 80, no. 3 (March 2001): 501–19.

5. Bodie, "A Racing Heart, Rattling Knees, and Ruminative Thoughts," *Communication Education*.

CHAPTER 8

1. YouGov, *New Year Survey: Fieldwork Dates: 8th–11th December 2017*, 2017, d25d2506sfb94s.cloudfront.net/cumulus_uploads/document/366cvmcg44/New%20Year%20Survey,%20December%208%2011,%202017.pdf.

2. Kelsey Mulvey, "80% of New Year's Resolutions Fail by February—Here's How to Keep Yours," *Business Insider*, January 3, 2017, businessinsider.com/new-year s-resolutions-courses-2016-12.

3. Sandro Sperandei, Marcelo C. Vieira, and Arianne C. Reis, "Adherence to Physical Activity in an Unsupervised Setting: Explanatory Variables for High Attrition Rates Among Fitness Center Members," *Journal of Science and Medicine in Sport* 19, no. 11 (November 2016): 916–20.

4. "Day in the Life: Simone Biles," *Owaves*, September 15, 2016, owaves.com/day-plans/day-life-simone-biles/.

5. Ralf Brand and Panteleimon Ekkekakis, "Affective-Reflective Theory of Physical Inactivity and Exercise," *German Journal of Exercise and Sport Research* 48, no. 6 (November 2018): 48–58.

6. Steven C. Hayes et al., "Acceptance and Commitment Therapy: Model, Processes and Outcomes," *Behaviour Research and Therapy* 44, no. 1 (January 2016): 1–25.

7. Alex Feary, "Case Study—Acceptance Commitment Therapy for a Youth Athlete: From Rumination and Guilt to Meaning and Purpose," *Sport and Exercise Psychology Review* 14, no. 1 (September 2018): 73–86.

8. Marleen Gillebaart and Denise T. D. de Ridder, "Effortless Self-Control: A Novel Perspective on Response Conflict Strategies in Trait Self-Control," *Social and Personality Psychology Compass* 9, no. 2 (February 2015): 88–99.

9. Wanda Wendel-Vos et al., "Potential Environmental Determinants of Physical Activity in Adults: A Systematic Review," *Obesity Reviews* 8, no. 5 (September 2007): 425–40.

10. Lisa Pridgeon and Sarah Grogan, "Understanding Exercise Adherence and Dropout: An Interpretative Phenomenological Analysis of Men and Women's Accounts of Gym Attendance and Non-attendance," *Qualitative Research in Sport, Exercise and Health* 4, no. 3 (August 2012): 382–99.

CHAPTER 9

1. D. A. Baden et al., "Effect of Anticipation During Unknown or Unexpected Exercise Duration on Rating of Perceived Exertion, Affect, and Physiological Function," *British Journal of Sports Medicine* 39, no. 10 (October 2005): 742–46.

2. Noel E. Brick et al., "Anticipated Task Difficulty Provokes Pace Conservation and Slower Running Performance," *Medicine and Science in Sports and Exercise* 51, no. 4 (April 2019): 734–43.

3. David Fletcher and Mustafa Sarkar, "Mental Fortitude Training: An Evidence-Based Approach to Developing Psychological Resilience for Sustained Success," *Journal of Sport Psychology in Action* 7, no. 3 (December 2016): 135–57.

CHAPTER 10

1. Meb Keflezighi with Scott Douglas, *Meb for Mortals: How to Run, Think, and Eat Like a Champion Marathoner* (New York: Rodale, 2015), 47.

2. Edward L. Deci and Richard M. Ryan, "*Self-Determination Theory*," in Handbook of Theories of Social Psychology, ed. Paul A. M. Van Lange, Arie W. Kruglanski, and E. Tory Higgins (London: Sage Publications, 2011), 416–36.

3. Kevin Filo, Daniel C. Funk, and Danny O'Brien, "Examining Motivation for Charity Sport Event Participation: A Comparison of Recreation-Based and Charity-Based Motives," *Journal of Leisure Research* 43, no. 4 (December 2011): 491–518.

CHAPTER 11

1. Nikos Ntoumanis et al., "Self-Regulatory Responses to Unattainable Goals: The Role of Goal Motives," *Self and Identity* 13, no. 5 (September 2014): 594–612.

2. James O. Prochaska et al., "Stages of Change and Decisional Balance for 12 Problem Behaviors," *Health Psychology* 13, no. 1 (January 1994): 39–46.

3. William R. Miller and Gary S. Rose, "Motivational Interviewing and Decisional Balance: Contrasting Responses to Client Ambivalence," *Behavioural and Cognitive Psychotherapy* 43, no. 2 (March 2015): 129–41.

4. Paschal Sheeran and Thomas L. Webb, "The Intention–Behavior Gap," *Social and Personality Psychology Compass* 10, no. 9 (September 2016): 503–18.

5. Gergana Y. Nenkov and Peter M. Gollwitzer, "Pre- Versus Postdecisional Deliberation and Goal Commitment: The Positive Effects of Defensiveness," *Journal of Experimental Social Psychology* 48, no. 1 (January 2012): 106–121.

CHAPTER 12

1. Paschal Sheeran and Thomas L. Webb, "The Intention–Behavior Gap," *Social and Personality Psychology Compass* 10, no. 9 (September 2016): 503–18.

2. Charles S. Carver, "Pleasure as a Sign You Can Attend to Something Else: Placing Positive Feelings within a General Model of Affect," *Cognition and Emotion* 17, no. 2 (March 2003): 241–61.

3. Carver, "Pleasure as a Sign You Can Attend to Something Else," *Cognition and Emotion.*

APPENDIX 1

1. Richard J. Butler and Lew Hardy, "The Performance Profile: Theory and Application," *Sport Psychologist* 6, no. 3 (September 1992): 253–64.

2. Neil Weston, Iain Greenlees, and Richard Thelwell, "A Review of Butler and Hardy's (1992) Performance Profiling Procedure Within Sport," *International Review of Sport and Exercise Psychology* 6, no. 1 (January 2013): 1–21.

3. Neil J. V. Weston, Iain A. Greenlees, and Richard C. Thelwell, "Athlete Perceptions of the Impacts of Performance Profiling," *International Journal of Sport and Exercise Psychology* 9, no. 2 (June 2011): 173–88.

4. Graham Jones, "The Role of Performance Profiling in Cognitive Behavioral Interventions in Sport," *Sport Psychologist* 7, no. 2 (June 1993): 160–72.

5. Daniel Gould and Ian Maynard, "Psychological Preparation for the Olympic Games," *Journal of Sports Sciences* 27, no. 13 (September 2009): 1393–408.

6. Nicola S. Schutte and John M. Malouff, "The Impact of Signature Strengths Interventions: A Meta-analysis," *Journal of Happiness Studies* 20, no. 4 (April 2019): 1179–96.

Acknowledgments

———

Noel and Scott would like to thank:

Nicholas Cizek and everyone else at The Experiment who believed in and helped to hone our book idea.

All the athletes who volunteered for our research and whom we've ever interviewed about their psychological strategies and techniques. Special thanks to Alvina Begay, Steve Holman, Meb Keflezighi, Lillian Kay Petersen, Kikkan Randall, and Brianna Stubbs.

Noel would also like to thank Holly Brick, his family, and his coauthor for his calming influence and guidance through what has been a challenging but enjoyable journey. He would also like to thank Ulster University for allowing him the time to focus on the process of writing this book.

Scott would also like to thank Stacey Cramp, Brian Dalek, and his coauthor for patience and support when book writing coincided with trying personal times that called for using every strategy in this book.

Index

NOTE: Page references in *italics* refer to charts and figures.

About the Authors

———

Noel Brick, PhD, is a British Psychological Society–chartered psychologist, a lecturer in sport and exercise psychology at Ulster University, and a researcher on the psychology of endurance performance. He has published research in the most prestigious sport and exercise science journals, such as *Medicine and Science in Sports and Exercise* (flagship journal of the American College of Sports Medicine) and *Psychology of Sport and Exercise* (flagship journal of the European Federation of Sport Psychology). He has presented his research at global academic conferences, including the annual congresses of the Association for Applied Sport Psychology, the British Psychological Society, the European College of Sport Science, and the European Federation of Sport Psychology. Noel has completed more than thirty marathons and ultramarathons. He is a native of Kerry and lives in County Antrim, Ireland.

noelbrick.com | @noelbrickie

SCOTT DOUGLAS is a contributing writer for *Runner's World*, and has held senior editorial positions at *Runner's World* and *Running Times*. He is the author or coauthor of several books, including *Running Is My Therapy*, *Advanced Marathoning*, and the *New York Times* bestsellers *Meb for Mortals* and *26 Marathons*. He has written about fitness and health for *Slate*, *The Atlantic*, *The Washington Post*, and *Outside*, among other outlets. Scott has run more than 100,000 miles since taking up the sport in 1979. He lives in South Portland, Maine.

scottdouglas.biz | @mescottdouglas